Real Life
Is a
Contact Sport

Real Life
Is A
Contact Sport

Designing Your Relationship Network

Bruce & Stan

VINE
BOOKS

SERVANT PUBLICATIONS
ANN ARBOR, MICHIGAN

Vine Books is an imprint of Servant Publications especially designed to serve evangelical
Christians.

Scripture quotations are taken from the *Holy Bible*, New Living Translation, © 1996. Used by
permission of Tyndale House Publishers, Inc., Wheaton, Illinois 60189. All rights reserved.

Published by Servant Publications
P.O. Box 8617
Ann Arbor, Michigan 48107

Cover design: Left Coast Design, Portland, Oregon
Cover illustration: Cecil Rice, Acworth, Georgia

00 01 02 03 10 9 8 7 6 5 4 3 2 1

Printed in the United States of America
ISBN 1-56955-199-5

Library of Congress Cataloging-in-Publication Data

Bickel, Bruce, 1952-
    Real life is a contact sport / Bruce & Stan.
        p.   cm.
    Includes bibliographical references.
    ISBN 1-56955-199-5 (alk. paper)
    1. Interpersonal relations—Religious aspects—Christianity.   I. Jantz, Stan, 1952-
    II. Title.
    BV4597.52.B53   2000
    248.4—dc21   00-042281

Contents

Introduction

With most sports, much of the enjoyment is lost if you are playing by yourself:

- If it's tennis, you can serve a lot of aces, but you never get the chance to volley.
- If it's soccer, it's easier to kick a goal if you're playing by yourself, but if the ball goes out of bounds there is no one to throw it back into play. You'll be standing around for a long time with your shorts flapping in the breeze.
- If it's bowling ... well, we aren't really sure if bowling is a sport. But even if it is, the best part about bowling is heckling your opponents with impolite comments about their form and style while munching on nachos or chili fries at that little scoring table.

Real life is the same way. Much of the enjoyment involves your interaction with other people. Oh, sure, you can get through a lot of life all by yourself, but it won't be the same, and neither will you.

Lost on the Information Superhighway?

With all of the technological advancements in our culture, it is possible to spend most of life insulated from other people in a societal cocoon.

- As your day starts, you can avoid other customers at Starbucks by using the drive-up window.
- If you purchase one of those cars manufactured in Yugoslavia, no one will want to carpool with you because the seats are so uncomfortable. (Of course, your morning commute will take a little longer because you

can't use the freeway's carpool express lane. But that's a small price to pay for the serenity of solitude.)

- At work, you can hibernate in your office with the door closed. If you haven't climbed the corporate ladder high enough to finagle a private office, then you will have to think of creative ways to keep people out of your cubicle. (We suggest draping that yellow police tape across the opening. However, the words "Do Not Cross – Crime Scene" may adversely affect your advancement in the company.)

- Eating lunch alone is easy. Just stay at your desk. The brown bag, the bologna sandwich, and the boxed juice drink are universally recognized symbols of anti-socials everywhere.

- And spending the evening at home alone is no problem either. That's the whole purpose of frozen dinners and video rentals. (But don't watch prime-time television. Most of those insipid programs are likely to drive you out of your house in search of intelligent life-forms.)

But this is no way to live. Before long, your life will be void of laughter—because you've heard all of your own jokes. You'll be stuck as your own best friend (and that's not good, because you'll find yourself to be pretty boring). And you'll also be your own worst enemy (and life is much easier if your frustrations are directed at someone other than yourself).

Something to think about: *Solitary confinement is used as the harshest penalty for convicted felons* (not counting the electric chair and gas chamber—which seem a little severe as personal lifestyle options). Although we don't know you very well (yet), we're hoping that any living arrangement suitable for Ted Kaczynski and Charles Manson is inappropriate for you.

On the Other Hand ...
Societal Overload Can Be Just As Bad

Our culture often seems to brand "loners" as "losers." So maybe you've gone a little overboard with your social contacts, cramming your Palm Pilot full of names, phone numbers, and E-mail addresses to stay "connected." Of course, you have to spread your time and attention among so many relationships that you can't get very close to any of them. You came to this shocking realization when:

- You sent out thirty-two E-mails and left twenty-seven voice mail messages, and still couldn't find anyone willing to help you move furniture into your new apartment last Saturday; or
- At the last three wedding receptions you've attended, you've been stuck at the table in the back next to some distant relative of the bride or groom who wants to sign you up in some multilevel marketing scheme; or
- After working hard to organize a ski trip weekend with sixteen friends, you told everyone to make their own carpooling arrangements. The next thing you know, everyone has piled into three cars … leaving you to drive seven hours with only skis, luggage, and Presto Logs to keep you company.

If you have too many acquaintances, you may find yourself with too few close friends.

It Really Is a Matter of "Who You Know"

You've heard that old adage, "It's not *what* you know, but *who* you know." Your professors in college probably scoffed at this notion. What did you expect? Their job is to teach you all about the "what" stuff. But it doesn't take a Mensa member to figure out that an uncle who owns a software company may be more helpful to your career than knowing the dates and the names of the ancient Chinese dynasties from your college World Civ class.

OK, we'll admit that "what" you know has some relevance and importance. (We'd rather have a surgeon who got good grades in medical school than one who made it through only because her dad was a rich alum who donated big bucks to the university.) But for most of real life, your circumstances are significantly impacted by "who" you know.

There are some obvious benefits to "cultivating" certain relationships and contacts. There is that friend of a friend who is moving out of a great condominium that you want to sublet. And then there's that neighbor of your cousin who is in charge of personnel at the company where you have applied for a high-paying job. A few well-timed personal recommendations on your behalf by your friend and your cousin in these circumstances could leave you sitting pretty. But your relationship network will affect your life in ways that go far beyond a condo and some cash:

- Your free-time activities are often decided by the people you hang out with. What you do and where you go are often the result of group decisions. (Hey, if you don't believe us, just ask any guy you see at a Jane Austen movie.)
- Your political, philosophical, and religious opinions are influenced, or at least tested, in the conversations at work and in social settings.
- Your goals and aspirations are often determined by the people you admire and who serve as your role models and mentors.
- Your sense of identity can be traced to your family (whether you are proud of your heritage or are trying to hide the fact that you ever swam in that gene pool).

What This Book Is All About

In a sense, this book is all about you. Or, to put it another way, it's about everybody *except* you. Confused? Don't be … we are just trying to illustrate one of the major points of this book:

Your Relationships Make a Difference in Your Life

The people in your circle of contacts—your "network" of relationships—all play a part in your development as a person.

> *The mental, social, physical, and*
> *spiritual dimensions of your life*
> *are not developed in an isolation chamber.*
> *They are forged in the crucible of social interaction.*

Wow, that was lofty. We usually don't get quite so esoteric. Instead, let's just say:

Other people—the ones you like and some you don't— play an influential part in your life.

There, that's more like it. We'll try not to let that esoteric thing happen again.

Unless you plan on living as a reclusive Bedouin in the Gobi hinterland, you're going to establish relationships with other people. It's a fact. Whether it occurs at work, or in your neighborhood, or at church, or in the other places you frequent on a regular basis, it will happen. Count on it.

The good news is that you don't have to be passive in the relationship-building process. That's another major point of this book:

Your Relationships Can Be Made by Default or by Design

Considering the long-lasting effect that your relationships will have on your life, you may want to give this important subject a little more attention.

We're Not Experts—We Don't Even Play Them on TV— So Why Should You Listen to Us?

Usually it is people with "Ph.D." after their names who write books about relationships. You won't find those initials after our names, though. (Bruce has "J.D." after his, which means he is a lawyer, which means you should be initially distrustful of anything he says. Stan received a "B.A." degree in college, which means he has mastered the first two letters of the alphabet—but not even in the right order.) So, why should you pay attention to what we have to say about relationships?

Good question.

We are cultural observers. (Do you like that description? We made it up ourselves.) We look at society in general, and people in particular, and we think about what they are doing. In many cases it's obvious that they're not thinking about it, and it seems like somebody should, so we have volunteered. But our analysis of cultural relationships is not limited to the concoctions from our own cranial capacities:

- We read a lot of the books written by those people with the Ph.D. initials;
- We both have strong connections with colleges (Bruce with Westmont College and Stan with Biola University), so we spend a lot of time with college and postcollege types who give us their input and insights;
- We know a little about relationships ourselves. Hey, we have written about twenty books together (and writing with a co-author can be more stressful than hanging wallpaper with a committee). We each have a long-term marriage that is solid (which is probably more a tribute to our wives than to ourselves).

But most important of all, we have discovered an ancient Middle-Eastern book filled with wisdom for the ages. From this book we have uncovered secrets to strong and lasting relationships. OK, the "ancient Middle-Eastern book" is the Bible. But don't discount its divinely inspired wisdom just because you can find this book in the bedside table of any Motel 6.

From time to time throughout this book, we will point you to what the Bible says about building relationships with others (as well as what it says about you). Since we don't even pretend to be experts, consider us as friends who are exploring this subject of relationships with you. We're just here to raise a few issues and help you think things through for yourself. We won't get condescending with you, and we won't be pedagogical or preachy. In fact, we recognize that you might have insights that we could learn from, so don't hesitate to tell us a thing or two. (See the "About the Authors" page at the back of the book for how to contact us.)

This book is all about you, people, and God (that covers just about everyone, doesn't it?). We've divided the book's twelve chapters into three parts. In Part I we'll look at you and what your real life is all about. In Part II we'll dig into the different dimensions of your relationship network—your family, your friends, the love of your life, your co-workers, those difficult people in your life, and your neighbors. And then in Part III we'll talk about how God fits into all of this.

Obviously, we are all interested in improving our lives and our relationships—or else we wouldn't have written this book, and you wouldn't be reading it. So dig in and have fun as you learn more about your real life.

What Are You Waiting For? Get Reading!

Hey! You aren't building relationships (or even learning about them) by reading this introduction. Time to take a bold step toward defining and designing your relationship network. Well, maybe it's not such a bold step. More like a baby step. Just turn the page and begin to read Chapter 1.

Part I

Your Real Life

Life is what happens to you
while you're busy making other plans.

John Lennon

The Wonderful World of Relationships

Neither of us is a professional athlete, but we enjoy sports (OK, we enjoy *watching* sports). If we were athletic, we would probably enjoy the elements of sports that make them fun and exciting: the competition, the excitement, the rivalry, and the physical exhilaration (hey, we're working up a sweat just *thinking* about sports).

Like you, we've watched everything from Little League games to big sports spectacles like the Super Bowl and the Olympics. We've come to the conclusion that sports and relationships have a lot in common. Pretty much everything you do to be successful in sports, whether you're a fierce competitor or a weekend warrior, you do to be successful in your relationships.

- You choose the sport carefully.
- You get into shape physically.
- You prepare yourself mentally.
- You develop your skills diligently.
- You control yourself emotionally.
- You discipline yourself regularly.

The bottom line to all this effort is that you want to be successful. As the old saying goes, it doesn't matter whether you win or lose; it's how you play the game. The same thing goes for your life and your life relationships.

Now, we're not going to spend a lot of time analyzing sports (mainly because we don't know a whole lot), but we do want to start off with some sports analogies to get the ball (and this book) rolling. Here are a few sports we've selected at random to help explain what we mean by the phrase *Real Life Is a Contact Sport*. See if you don't see some parallels between these different sports and the different ways people relate to each other:

Golf. Golf is hot right now for one very simple reason: Tiger Woods. He has all it takes—precocious skill, amazing concentration, and a fierce competitive spirit. He stays cool under pressure and knows how to come from behind to win. Tiger conquers a golf course one hole at a time.

Some people treat relationships like golf. With great precision they take their relationships one at a time. Their goal is to get to each pin in fewer shots than their competitors.

Football. Football is more of a team sport, and it's not for the faint of heart. Like the military, it's all about guts and glory. The teams are heavily armored as they march down the field to take enemy territory in a predetermined amount of time.

Sometimes people handle relationships like they're marking and capturing territory. They mask their true feelings, put on lots of emotional padding, and always set out to take the upper hand.

Baseball. Baseball is also a team sport, but it's much more relaxed than football. There's no time limit, and you don't need any serious padding. Instead of a helmet, you put on a cap (it's hard to look tough in a cap). And rather than marching into the other team's end zone, you simply cross home plate.

When it comes to relationships, some people act like baseball players. They'll hustle if necessary, but mostly they like relaxing on the sidelines with a mouthful of sunflower seeds, occasionally engaging in relationship "chatter" as the game of life goes by.

Hockey. The goal of hockey always seems to be conflict. Smashing your opponent into the sideboard is almost as good as scoring a goal. And what's a hockey game without at least one good fight?

Some people go through life like they're in a hockey game, ready to pick a verbal fight with anyone who gets in the way.

Soccer. We admit it, we have a hard time getting excited about soccer. The teams spend most of the time simply kicking the ball back and forth, rarely scoring a goal.

Soccer is a great metaphor for many relationships these days. People run around a lot, relating to a bunch of different people, saying very little and accomplishing even less. On the whole, it's pretty frustrating (kind of like watching a soccer game).

Curling. Hey, don't laugh. Here's a sport (almost) in which everyone works together to slide a disc-shaped stone along a slippery path into a goal area (we're not terribly sure about the terminology, but you get the idea). Nobody's shoving, spitting, fighting, or standing idly by. Everyone contributes in some way.

Now, that's the way relationships should work. Our vote for the best sport metaphor for a solid, successful relationship network is curling. See what we mean?

You can find all kinds of analogies between sports and relationships. And think about this: if you applied the same kind of dedication and energy and discipline to your relationships as you do to your involvement in sports, how much better would your life be?

What Do We Know?

At this point in the book, you have already come to a couple of conclusions. First, you realize that we don't know a whole lot about sports. Second, you're pretty sure that we weren't exaggerating when we said we aren't "relationship experts." That is, we have no professional credentials such as degrees in psychology, sociology, or theology.

And yet you have decided to give this book a try, which can only mean one of two things. Either you're ready for a refreshing look at relationships from two ordinary guys who are basically just like you (except you're probably more normal and better looking). Or you've considered the alternatives, and you just don't want to read a book on relationships by ...

- A radio talk show host who berates people for their stupid mistakes,
- A pop psychologist who uses planets to describe human characteristics,
- An energetic guy with large teeth who says that if you want to be a popular, good-looking zillionaire like him, all you have to do is look within yourself,
- A diminutive doctor who believes the secret of any relationship is found in sex (but not with her).

So here you are, ready to find out what "these two guys" (that would be us) have to say about something that's very important to you (that would be relationships).

The truth is, even though we have no credentials, we really do know something about relationships—and so do you. We can't help it. We're human beings surrounded by other human beings living in a world populated by human beings.

You've been experiencing human interactions for as long as you have been alive, and so you already know some things about how to relate to other people. Let's pull out that knowledge, combine it with ours, and pool it into a set of propositions about relationships. Let's call it—

Ten Things We Know for Sure About Relationships

1. You can't live without relationships. OK, this one is a no-brainer, but we have to include it in our Top Ten list, because some people have the strange notion that you can get along perfectly well in life without relationships ...

I love mankind—it's people I can't stand.
Charlie Brown

... but it's impossible! From the day you were born, when a doctor with cold hands released you from the cozy confines of your mother's womb, you have had to depend on other people for your very existence. Even now that you aren't a kid anymore, you're not totally independent. Here's what we mean:

- When you were a baby, someone had to *feed* you. As an adult, you still need people to feed you—farmers, food processors, grocers, and McDonald's servers.
- As a baby, someone had to *change* you and clean up after you. Hey, guess what? You may be doing most of the work, but you still depend on others—plumbers, sanitation engineers, and waste disposal people.
- When you were a baby, someone had to *dress* you. Hey, baby, you may pick out your wardrobe in the morning, but other people had to grow the material, manufacture your threads, sell you the goods, and give you a job so you could buy your favorite cotton clothing from the Gap. If they hadn't, you'd be buck-naked (and not as cute and cuddly as you were at the beginning of your life).

You may not know all of these people, but you need them. You may not relate to them, but you depend on them. Think about that next time you take that minimum wage French-fryer for granted. You need that guy—acne and all!

"Maslow's Hierarchy of Needs"

If you've taken Psychology 101, you know all about Abraham Maslow's "hierarchy of needs." We're not saying it is gospel truth, but most of the world buys into this approach to the human condition and its effect on relationships.

So here's the theory, in a nutshell. Everyone has certain levels of need, with each level building on the previous one. In other words, if you don't satisfy one level, the theory goes, you can't move on to the next.

Physiological Needs. The lowest level on Maslow's hierarchy includes our basic biological needs such as oxygen, food, water, and shelter. If these needs aren't met, you die. (continued on next page)

> **Safety Needs.** A little higher up on Maslow's model is our need for security. We all have a need to feel safe, whether as children or adults. And we all have the need to *be* safe from dangerous elements, whether animal, vegetable, or mineral—raging rhinos, killer tomatoes (technically a fruit, not a vegetable), or acid rain.
>
> **Love, Affection, and the Need to Belong.** Everyone has the need to escape loneliness and to receive (as well as give) love, affection, and the sense of belonging.
>
> **Esteem Needs.** We have the need for a stable and fairly high level of self-respect, as well as the respect of others. According to Maslow, if these needs are not met, we feel inferior, weak, and worthless.
>
> **Self-Actualization Needs.** This is the highest tier on Maslow's tower, the level in which human beings realize their full potential through an ongoing process of being devoted to a cause or a calling. When we reach this level, we find meaning, because we are doing what we were born to do.

2. Sometimes you can't live *with* relationships. It's a given that you need people—usually people you don't know real well—to take care of your basic needs. You don't have to get to know them on a deeper level because you don't see them all that often. But what about the people you do see almost every day—your family, your close friends, your co-workers, and your neighbors?

In that mix there are going to be some people you like to be around, but there are also going to be some people you can't stand: annoying people, obnoxious people, demanding people, *difficult* people. You'd like to get away from them, but that would be impossible, because they're your brother-in-law, your boss, your next-door neighbor, or your roommate. These are the relationships you can't live with, but you have to.

There may be times when you'd like nothing better than to get out from under the demands, pressures, expectations, and strange habits of these people, but you know you've got to figure out a way to deal with them.

3. Relationships can be incredibly rewarding. OK, let's talk about the positive side of relationships. Nothing on earth has the capacity to bring you joy and fulfillment like a wonderful relationship, especially when it's with those people in your life who have brought you incredible joy and fulfillment—

Factoid

In 1970 around ten million people fifteen years of age or older lived alone. Today more than twenty-five million people live alone.

- Your mother, who loves you no matter what,
- Your father, who has been patient with you despite your mistakes,
- Your best friend in the world, who would do anything you ask,
- Your husband or wife, with whom you have developed a relationship that words can't describe,
- Your child, for whom you would give your life if you had to.

These are the kinds of people who make relationships the greatest gift in the world.

4. Relationships can bring a lot of pain. There's something else we all know about relationships. When they go bad, there's nothing more painful. A sour relationship usually means you've been hurt or betrayed in some way. A person you care very much about stabbed you in the back or did something that brought you great disappointment.

And then there are those relationships that you messed up and those people you disappointed. Sometimes the burden of being the one at fault is just as overwhelming. Often the pain of knowing you can't do anything to make it right is more than you can bear.

Regardless of who caused the pain, when you go through a negative relationship experience, you may be reluctant to forgive or ask forgiveness—and that's no fun for anyone.

5. When conflict arises, it's usually the other person's fault. We're not saying this is always true, but it's usually the way we feel. It's human nature to want to place the blame for conflict on the other person.

> *God:* Hey, Adam, did you eat the apple I told you not to eat?
> *Adam:* Uh, yeah, but it was that woman you gave me who brought me the fruit, so I ate it.

But that doesn't make it right. Why are we so quick to blame the other person, when at least half the time (if you're a man, more than half the time) it's our own fault? And even when it's not our problem, why don't we try to see the situation from the other person's point of view?

If a man says something in the forest, and there's no one around to hear him, he's still wrong.

All Women

---

6. The other person feels the same way. Before we blame someone else for a problem, we might as well try to see it from the other person's viewpoint, because that's the way he or she is seeing it.

> *God:* So, Eve, Adam tells me you gave him the apple. How could you do such a thing?
> *Eve:* It was that stupid snake. He tricked me, and that's why I ate it.

Now, the "other person" may not always be right, but as long as *he* (or she) thinks he's right, no amount of arguing in the world is going to change his mind. Besides, you may discover (and if you're mature enough, you'll admit it) that the other person is right—sort of. And even if he's not, he will appreciate your willingness to listen.

7. It's natural to want to "take" from your relationships. As long as we're being honest, let's admit something we all know about ourselves: we're needy. As we have already discussed, we started needing stuff the day we were born. We need food, shelter, clothing, and all those other things at the bottom of Maslow's hierarchy.

On the other hand, assuming that you're not living in a cardboard box or driving a Yugo, your need for the physical stuff is far outweighed by your need for the emotional stuff (the stuff at the top part of Maslow's hierarchy). This is what you're looking for in relationships. The trouble is, people don't automatically supply your emotional needs. Unlike a job where you know in advance that a certain quantity of work can be exchanged for a set amount of money, you can't just take your charming personality to someone's emotional bank and expect to withdraw love, affection, and esteem. So you take what you can.

8. When it comes to relationships, it's better to give than to take. There have been times in your life when you have done something for someone else just for the sheer pleasure of doing it, with no expectations that you would get anything in return—and it was the greatest feeling in the world. One of the greatest things we know about relationships—and you know it, too—is that it really is better to give than to receive. We're not talking about giving gifts, but giving out of your emotional bank rather than always taking from others.

9. We all bring baggage to our relationships. Boy, could we write a book (and so could you). No, not this book, but a book about our lives—where we were born, the families we were born into, the experiences we have had, the people we've known.

Think about your life for a minute. You didn't just pop up in a vacuum. Your life is the product of years of moments, made up of millions of impressions recorded in the incredible memory mechanism of your brain. You've got a unique set of DNA—thanks to your parents and their parents (and so forth). But the personality you were born with has been strongly influenced by the family you grew up with—whether functional or dysfunctional, funny or serious, carefree or driven, God-centered or not God-centered—along with the friends you've made and all the people you've met.

Whenever you are relating to another person at any given moment, you need to picture both of you standing there with full sets of Samsonite luggage at your feet. This isn't a bad thing. It's the way things are. All of us have been influenced and shaped by our past relationships. The good news is that we have the opportunity to shape our future relationships by designing our relationship network.

10. One of the biggest fears of any relationship is commitment. We've saved this observation about relationships for last, because it's the biggest stumbling block for moving forward in healthy and productive relationships. The issue of commitment used to be a sign of strength. When two people wanted to forge a deeper relationship, they made a commitment to each other. These days, due to our fear of rejection and failure, we are reluctant to commit to any type of relationship at any level.

Take marriage as an example. Traditionally marriage has been seen as the ultimate blending of two human beings into a single glorious relationship. The words "marital" and "bliss" used to go together like "horse" and "carriage." But in the last few decades, the institution of marriage has taken a beating. Couples are reluctant to commit to a relationship they know will change their lives forever—for better or for worse.

In 1970 the median age of men marrying for the first time was twenty-three, and for women it was twenty-one. Today the age is twenty-seven for men and twenty-five for women.

It's not just marriage that scares people off. Men and women alike are afraid to commit to all kinds of relationships, including basic friendships.

Are You Relationally Homeless?

So far we've established that we know a lot more about relationships than we realize simply because we have been relating to people all of our lives. But does that mean we're good at it? Not necessarily.

In his book *Relationships That Work*, Dr. H. Norman Wright says that even though relationships are all around us, "not all of us have experienced significant relationships." He writes that some people think they're in relationships, when they're really in "situations." That's because they aren't relating to people in a way that defines a relationship.

**For a relationship to exist there has to be "mutuality."
Each person has to make some contribution for
the relationship to exist. Both need to participate
in some way or it won't work.**

H. Norman Wright

People who skip around from one person to the next without being genuine with anyone are what Dr. Wright calls "relationally homeless." They're like the guy who channel surfs (we can relate) without watching anything. Relationally homeless people never stay with one person long enough to really connect.

Nobody sets out to be relationally homeless, just like nobody decides one day, "You know, I'm tired of living in one place. I think I'll leave home, make a cardboard sign, and sit next to a street light, hoping people will take pity on me." But it happens in the real homeless world, and it happens in the world of relationships.

By refusing to commit to anyone on more than a superficial level, for whatever reason, soon you will find security in your little relationally homeless life. And there you are, on a street corner with your pathetic little cardboard sign that says, "I don't know you and you don't know me, so let's just leave it that way."

Are you relationally homeless? If you can't name at least one significant relationship with someone who is absolutely real with you—and you with them—then you are.

Why Some People Are Alone

There are two categories of relationally homeless people.

Alone by choice. The first group is made up of people who are relationally homeless by choice. Like the homeless guy who chooses to be homeless because he doesn't like the alternative, there are certain people who just don't want to relate to other people (at least that's the way they act).

Within this category of relationally homeless people are four different subcategories of people whom we've conveniently modeled after actual homeless people we have met as we've traveled around the country:

• *The disgruntled homeless guy.* This person is homeless and unhappy (as opposed to happy homeless people, who actually do exist). You've met relationally homeless people like this. They're basically unhappy, but don't try to change them. They are content—in fact, they find strength—in their unhappiness.

• *The dishonest homeless guy.* Have you ever seen a homeless person in his twenties holding a sign that says, "Please Help—Vietnam Vet"? Like he's fooling you and everyone else. You've also met relationally homeless people who are so obviously fake that the only way to relate would be to give them a dollar so they could buy a clue.

• *The demanding homeless guy.* Here's the street person with an attitude. You owe him a handout, and he's going to make you feel like dirt if you don't fork over some coin. This guy is no different than certain people who demand your friendship. They make you feel like you owe them a relationship, which of course you don't.

• *The disgusting homeless guy.* This is a guy who needs a bath and some dental work in the worst way (as opposed to a clean homeless guy with fine teeth). Some relationally homeless people could use some grooming tips, but mostly the disgust comes from their foul mouths or nasty attitudes.

Alone by circumstance. Most people don't fit any of the above categories (thank goodness). Most of the relationally homeless aren't alone because they're disgruntled, dishonest, demanding, or disgusting. They're nice people. They want friends, but for some reason they have trouble making and keeping friends. They know a lot of people, and really want to connect with just a few, but for some reason no one wants to get close to them.

These are the second category of the relationally homeless. These are the lonely people. We all know people like this, and if we were honest, we would have to admit that all of us have been lonely at some point in our lives—perhaps more than we'd care to admit.

Why does this happen? It's pointless to blame others for our loneliness, so the place we have to start is with ourselves. In *The Friendship Factor* (a book we highly recommend), Dr. Alan McGinnis lists several characteristics that will drive people away from you faster than the plague. See if you can identify with any of these.

• *The tendency to* **control** *others.* Dr. McGinnis writes that this personality trait "gets the prize for ruining more relationships than any other." It is a characteristic found to some degree in each of us, but when it gets out of hand, it is always destructive and always pushes people away.

• *The tendency to* **criticize** *others.* There's nothing wrong with constructive criticism if it's delivered at the right time and in the right spirit. But too much of our criticism is self-serving and spiteful. We criticize to hinder others, not help them.

• *The tendency to* **conform** *to others.* Have you ever had a friend who changed from the person you once knew? It's unsettling. We want our friends to stay the same, and let's admit it, to be a little like us. But if we hold on too tightly to conformity, it can damage a friendship. Especially when our friends change for the better—we can feel like we're being left behind.

• *The tendency to* **confine** *others.* Jealousy is at the heart of this tendency. It's easy to get nervous when the people we know (especially the people we know best), develop other friendships. Rather than let them go, we try to confine them.

Now, chances are that you aren't alone by choice or by circumstance, but you do find yourself in those lonely moments when you wonder why you can't build deeper and more satisfying relationships. You may have lots of friends—you might even be married—but you can't seem to move from casual to more meaningful connections.

It may be too simple to suggest that your tendency to control, criticize, conform, and confine others is the problem. All of us are capable of these tendencies at one time or another. But if they dominate your personality, this may be a good place to start.

Where Do We Go From Here?

We hope you don't mind that we started this book off rather negatively. Actually, we have two reasons for doing this. First, we have nowhere to go but up. Now that we've talked about what we know about relationships, including all the junk, we can move on to the good stuff. We can start down the path to healthy relationships, which come from making the right choices.

Second, none of us is exempt from negative qualities. By our very natures, we are self-serving and self-protecting. But we can improve the way we relate to people if we are willing to change and open to new ideas.

There are a lot of places you can look for ideas on how to choose good relationships and design a quality relationship network. Some are good, some not so good. In the next chapter we're going to look at some of the not-so-good places, which are primarily found in the media. Don't worry, we won't get negative on you. We're just going to help you sort through the signals and think through the messages the media delivers twenty-four hours a day, seven days a week.

CHAPTER 2

Real Life Is More
Than a Sitcom

You already know a lot about what you expect from relationships in your mental memory banks. That's part of the problem. We'll bet that your expectations are way off from your reality. We think the disparity (the difference between your expectations and your reality) may be caused by your source of information.

You are a member of the information age (unless you are in the population segment that is receiving Social Security or thinking about it). Whether you have been called part of Generation X or the Millennial Generation, the point is that you get most of your information and impressions about life from electronic impulses: signals that travel mysteriously (at least to us) through the air or wires to reach your television screen, your computer monitor, your cell phone, or your radio speakers.

When your grandparents were kids, they learned about life by listening to the adults talk at the dinner table; their exposure to the outside world was limited to the other families on the block, and maybe catching Walter Cronkite on the television news (in black and white). It was a pretty sheltered existence. But not so with you:

- You've always had CNN to give you up-to-the-minute details of note-worthy events from around the world as they happened (of course, your television was probably on the MTV channel during most of the historic events of the last century).
- *USA TODAY* has given you a graphics-loaded introduction to the people of our nation and our planet that is much more thorough than what you might receive by reading your Hometown Gazette (which is mostly useful for the ten-cents-off coupon for Kleenex at Hometown Pharmacy).
- The weekly issues of *People* and *Glamour* magazines have kept you up-to-date with what's happening in the world of fashion and celebrity romance. (Those on a budget might have had to resort to glancing at the *National Enquirer* headlines while standing in line at the super-market.)

But perhaps you have been influenced most by the entertainment industry: television, movies, and music. Think about it:

- You can sing all of the words to your favorite hit song, but you stumble over the lyrics of the national anthem.
- You can't remember the names of any justice on the United States Supreme Court, but you can recite the last five movies that won the Oscar for best picture.
- And you know all of the names of the characters from your favorite sit-com, but you can't remember your mother's maiden name when you're filling out a credit application.

The danger of all of this overexposure to the entertainment culture is that you will start to expect your life to resemble a sitcom. Don't let that happen. The relationships that you will have in real life aren't anything like what you will find on TV, at Blockbuster, or in an MTV music video.

Who Do You Think You Are?

It is quite possible that the sheer exposure to a daily average of 3.7 hours of television viewing, plus a few movies a month, has altered your sense of reality about who you are. Your view of other people might be equally skewed. Here are a few examples of what we mean (along with our cautionary advice if you have unwittingly bought into the media mentality).

Movie Mentalities ...

If you base your expectations about yourself and members of the opposite sex on what you see in the movies, you're going to be surprised, shocked, and probably disappointed with real life. In an effort to be of service to you (and to justify taking a tax deduction for our movie tickets), we have analyzed the male and female leading roles in recent movies. We have discovered that Hollywood promotes three basic (and unrealistic) character types for men and women. We will summarize each of the types for you, and (at no additional charge) we'll give you some cautionary advice just in case you are buying in to the Hollywood hype.

Male Stereotypes	Female Stereotypes
Guy Type #1: Adam Sandler	**Gal Type #1: Drew Barrymore**
This kind of guy is slightly wacky, fiercely independent, but always loveable. He may never amount to anything in the business world, but that's OK because he can get through life with his winsome sense of humor.	Basically the Adam Sandler type with an extra "X" chromosome. Like the characters portrayed by Ms. Barrymore, this woman is spirited, independent, and infectiously wild. She's fun-loving, cranked up a notch.
Reality Check. If you think of yourself as this kind of guy (or if you are attracted to him), try to imagine any of the Adam Sandler-type characters when they are fifty years old, still wearing a hockey shirt and making wisecracks in the unemployment line. At twenty-eight this is considered individualistic, but at age fifty it's pathetic.	*Reality Check:* If you're a gal, don't expect to be like this; and if you are a guy, stop looking for this type of woman. This type of character doesn't exist. Nobody could maintain this delicate balance between legality and lunacy. In the real world, this type of lifestyle usually involves a cell (of the barred or padded variety).

Male Stereotypes

Guy Type #2: Kevin Costner

The attraction most women have for this guy is based partly on his good looks, but more so on his intensive introspection. This guy has *feelings*, and he doesn't mind letting them show. In fact, he flaunts them.

Reality Check: If you are a gal, don't spend your time looking for this kind of guy—because he doesn't exist (except for Kevin Costner in real life). If you are a guy who imagines himself to be like Kevin Costner—wait, what are we saying? No guy would ever imagine himself like this.

Guy Type #3: Keanu Reeves

This guy can do it all. He's a unique blend of muscle, mind, and magnetism. But just so he won't be too perfect, this type of guy always has a bad haircut.

Reality Check: If you think the Keanu Reeves type is for you, first you must remember that there won't always be some catastrophic danger to add to the romance. In real life, guys with a brain avoid dangerous situations like they avoid feelings. And if you are a guy who fancies himself as the Keanu Reeves type, then get a clue and realize that your only similarity is the bad haircut.

Female Stereotypes

Gal Type #2: Julia Roberts

This natural beauty knows how to get what she wants with her womanly wiles. (Actually, we aren't sure what "wiles" are, but this type of woman knows how to use them.) Her sexual appeal is enhanced by a combination of sophistication and street smarts.

Reality Check: Don't get hung up on that "womanly wiles" thing. If you carefully analyze those Julia Roberts characters, you'll find that they really only have one thing in common: big teeth. So, if you're a gal, schedule a visit at the orthodontist's office. If you're a guy looking for this womanly type #2, apply for a job as the orthodontist's appointment secretary.

Gal Type #3: Meg Ryan

Smart but not arrogant. Cute but not conceited. Tender but not fragile. Romantic but not overly sentimental. Quirky but not demented. Funny but not raucous.

Reality Check: Hollywood tries to make you believe that this is the "girl next door." Yeah, sure—but only if you live in Tom Hanks' neighborhood. If you are a gal, don't pressure yourself to aspire to such flawless perfection. (Not even Meg Ryan can live up to the characters that she plays.) If you're a guy, don't think that such a gal is within your reach (unless you're like Tom Hanks—which you aren't).

Prime-Time Pitfalls ...

Even if you avoid the movies, your impression of "normal" isn't going to be any healthier or more realistic if your opinion about yourself and others is based on what you see on television.

On television the distinctions between the sexes blur; the categories become generic without gender differentiation. Whether a male or female, people are cast into one of three character classifications:

TV Type #1: Comic

A wisecracking clown who keeps you laughing with pratfalls and malapropisms. Romantic relationships are often limited for this type of person, but he or she is always surrounded by friends.

Reality Check: Using these television characters as role models won't work. Nobody is always this funny—especially the actors who play these roles (as proven by their insufferable interviews with Leno and Letterman). There is no one more pathetic than a wannabe jokester—and there is no one lonelier.

TV Type #2: Caustic

An antagonistic individual whose bitter remarks usually mask a tender heart. Every other episode or so, the gruff exterior crumbles and those suppressed inner passions are released in a tender and meaningful relationship.

Reality Check: If you think that you can get away with being rude, forget it. Nobody is going to stick around to find the tender "inner you." In real life, sarcastic people with their acerbic comments don't do well, except as political analysts.

TV Type #3: Conscientious

These are thoughtful, introspective people who take their professions very seriously, to the exclusion of romantic interests. This dedication apparently makes them attractive to the opposite sex.

Reality Check: In real life, there is a word to describe people with pensive and workaholic proclivities: boring. Oh, this might be an attractive trait for a doctor or a lawyer on those prime-time dramas. But outside the studio emergency room or courtroom set, you'll never hear anyone say: "Let's hang out with him. He works so hard and is so morose."

Musical Misperceptions ...

Even if you avoid movies and network television, you can still have major misconceptions about yourself and others. If you like music, and if you watch MTV, these misconceptions can creep into your mind by osmosis.

After any extended exposure to the music videos on this cable channel, you'll be under the mistaken impression that all women are tall and slender, and wear leather pants as they captivate men with sensual songs, double-jointed body movements, and low-cut necklines that reveal lots of cleavage. You'll think the same about men, minus the cleavage.

"Seinfeld": A Microcosm of Sitcom Society

Sitcom characters can become a part of real life. If you don't think so, just hang out around the coffee machine in the breakroom where you work (or, if you have a home office, go to Starbucks some morning and eavesdrop). You'll notice that many of the conversations revolve around the antics of the characters of last night's sitcoms. You'll hear people talking about the characters as if they were real people.

Do your part to protect society from this fallacy. Stride into the middle of the room and shout:

"The actors are real people, but the characters are not. It's all 'make-believe' and it's not real life. Wake up and smell the coffee!"

Then get ready to duck. It's likely that you'll become the target of coffee-cup-shaped projectiles, hurled at your head by the people who have formed sentimental attachments to their favorite sitcom characters. To challenge the reality of those characters is to question the existence of your co-workers (or the other customers at Starbucks who apparently don't have a real job either—or else they'd be at work).

If the characters in sitcoms were real people, you wouldn't want them as your friends. Oh, they manage to be engaging on television, but that is only because the situations are contrived by a group of scruffy writers. (Writers, we might add, who have no social life of their own because they are locked in a conference room for most of the year—being released and exposed to the light of day only when the show is on summer hiatus. So it shouldn't surprise you if the characters and situations don't resemble real life.)

Sitcom characters don't make ideal candidates for your friends (and are even less desirable as role models for you). Allow us to demonstrate our point. To do so, we'll analyze the most popular sitcom of the last decade: "Seinfeld."

We know you're familiar with the show. You watched it when it was in prime time, and you've seen it in syndication. While we are the first to admit that "Seinfeld" contributed some great phrases to our vernacular vocabulary, it lowered expectations for social relationships to a pathetic level. Picture in your mind that eclectic group of friends (Jerry, Elaine, George, and Kramer), and we'll show you what we mean.

You don't have to think very long to find the one word that defines the essence of each character: self-centeredness. In fact, the final show (a two-episode special) was a retrospective of clips (excuse us, "scenes") from their lives where they had acted selfishly and in complete disregard to others.

- *Kramer:* Face it, you couldn't last nine seasons with him barging into your apartment and eating out of your refrigerator.
- *George:* You already have too many friends who are cheap or jobless. You don't need one who is both.
- *Elaine:* She's gregarious all right, but you'd soon tire of listening to her talk only about herself.
- *Jerry:* He was the most "normal" character in the group, but you'll have to rule him out, too, because he wouldn't want you as one of his friends.

And Now, a Word From Our Sponsor

Did you ever wonder how these egotistical characters happened to remain friends for all those years? Think about it. They didn't stay together all of that time out of loyalty or devotion to each other. In fact, their lack of commitment to each other was usually the basis for the humor in each episode. They weren't nice to each other most of the time. But somehow, they stayed closely connected with nothing more than a shallow friendship. How can that be?

Our in-depth analysis uncovered the secret "something" that forged a bond of friendship among these four otherwise self-centered individuals. The cohesive element? Simple: commercial sponsors. Don't think that you can pull off a long-term friendship like the "Seinfeld" group. It is highly unlikely that you'll find corporate sponsors willing to pay you millions just to mention their names every once in a while.

The Hangout

Every group likes a place to hang out, and the "Seinfeld" gang was no different. So each episode would find them around the table at the coffee shop, a place where they could be totally unproductive. It wasn't a homeless shelter where they could be helping the less fortunate. Nope. The coffee shop was a very appropriate place for this self-absorbed group. It gave them a place where they could talk about themselves and gossip about others.

The Job

None of the "Seinfeld" characters ever revealed a sense of job satisfaction. None of them seemed to find a sense of purpose in an occupation. Just the opposite. If you were to formulate your impressions about jobs and the working world based on "Seinfeld," you would consider a career as something to be avoided rather than pursued.

- *Kramer:* He never had a job. Oh, he was always concocting some money-making plan, but they never worked out, and they never involved actual employment.
- *George:* When he was employed, he was always scheming for ways to avoid actually doing any work.
- *Elaine:* Her jobs, and particularly the people she worked with, were annoyances to her.
- *Jerry:* He had a job as a stand-up comedian. It must be a highly lucrative profession, because you never saw him performing (except in the opening and closing credits for the first few seasons of the show).

Their Families

Grandpa Walton must have been turning in his grave with every "Seinfeld" broadcast. There are no close-knit family gatherings, like the Waltons enjoyed. Family members of the "Seinfeld" cast (especially their parents) were a constant source of stress and irritation. Parents dispensed more guilt than wisdom, and were frequently subjects of derision by their children.

Now, we must be honest and admit that we enjoyed the humor of those parental characters (especially George's parents, Frank and Estelle). Hey, they put the "fun" in dysfunctional. But if you were to base your impressions and expectations of family life on "Seinfeld," you'd move as far away from your parents as possible (or start collecting nursing home brochures).

The Dates

The four major characters on "Seinfeld" (and basically all of their friends) were single. While marriage was discussed from time to time, it was always treated as something to be avoided (especially during the season that George was engaged) or something unobtainable. So, each episode usually involved a new girlfriend for Jerry, a new boyfriend for Elaine, a new disaster for George, or a new kook for Kramer.

There was good news and bad news for any actor asked to play one of these boyfriend or girlfriend roles on "Seinfeld":

- *First, the Good News:* "Seinfeld" had high Nielson ratings, so this guest spot meant great exposure.
- *Now, the Bad News:* The gig would last only one episode, since none of the "Seinfeld" characters could keep a relationship going for more than a week. (Our editor, Heidi Saxton, challenged our analysis on this point. She cited George's fiancée, Susan, and Elaine's boyfriend, Putty, as two examples of long-term relationships on the show. Well, Heidi is correct that those *actors* were the exception to the one-episode rule, but the relationships with those *characters* were still short-lived. George wanted out of the engagement on the same episode in which he proposed, and Elaine and Putty would break up and reconcile several times on the same episode. So, Heidi, keep your day job and leave the in-depth sitcom analysis to us "Seinfeld" junkies.)

All dating relationships on "Seinfeld" had two common elements:

1. *Short-term expectations.* No one expected any relationship to have long-term potential. Faultfinding was often the mechanism used in these

relationships to provide comedic relief—and squash any long-term potential.

2. *Relationships were established primarily for the purpose of sexual gratification.* Every time two people started dating, there was sexual action—or at least lots of talk about it—before the next commercial break.

The duration of these short-term relationships (the average being eighteen minutes, excluding commercials) was one of the few realistic aspects of the show. It doesn't take a radio psychologist to explain that relationships with self-centered, shallow individuals won't last long. And it doesn't take a mathematician to figure out that "Seinfeld" concluded after nine seasons only because Jerry had dated all of the attractive women in New York.

Don't Pull the Plug!

Don't get us wrong. We like TV. In fact, there are some shows that we love, and "Seinfeld" is one of them. So we aren't saying that you shouldn't watch TV. Hey, you'll be living in cultural isolation if you don't at least channel surf from time to time. (For example, you'll find this last discussion pointless if you haven't had sufficient exposure to "Seinfeld.")

We're just saying that you shouldn't get sucked into the notion that sitcoms are a reflection of real life. They aren't. But you can use them as an impetus to start thinking critically and deliberately about who you are going to allow in your network of relationships. Jerry let Kramer barge through the door and open the refrigerator and cupboards without restraint. You should be a little more discriminating with those you let enter your life.

Ten Important Differences
Between Real Life and Sitcom Life

We know it may be difficult for you to admit that life on sitcoms does not reflect reality. Your mom was probably watching "The Mary Tyler Moore Show" while you were being breast-fed, so it has been absorbed into your system.

Before you can do any serious thinking about your life and your relationships, you'll have to wean yourself off the notion that sitcoms are a reflection of real life. Perhaps we can help with that weaning process. (That would make us the weanors, and you the weanie.) Here are ten ways in which real life is drastically different from life as portrayed on the sitcoms:

1. In real life you won't always be the star. If your life were a sitcom, then all the attention would center on you. You would be the focus of every situation. From the opening "scene" in the morning to the final "scene" at night, the attention of everyone in the world would be riveted on you and your life. You have probably already discovered that real life isn't like that.

Yes, there is a lot about you in your life, but there is also a lot about other people. The spotlight won't always be on you. Sometimes in life you have to work behind the scenes. Sometimes your name won't even be on the credits at the end of the show (or the print may be so small that it will roll across the screen too fast for anyone to notice that you were the second assistant to the guy who drove the food catering truck).

If you are expecting that you are going to be the "star of the show" in the program of your life, you're going to be in for a major disappointment. Your life involves an ensemble cast. (More about that in Part II.)

2. In real life, there are no scriptwriters. Sitcom characters are popular because they manage to be funny all of the time. Well, it's easy for them— they have scriptwriters. You don't, and therein lies a huge difference between sitcom life and real life.

In real life, you won't always be funny. Your friends won't always be funny, either. In real life, situations will require you to talk seriously about subjects and to talk about subjects that are serious.

Real life doesn't have a laugh track. Don't think that you need to be changing the channel on your relationships just because you can't hear a constant roar of giggles and guffaws in the background.

3. In real life, your conflicts won't end in thirty minutes. Sitcom characters aren't perfect friends. They mess up and offend each other. Even if a conflict is serious, it always manages to be made right before the final commercial.

We can pretty much guarantee that your conflicts will have a lifespan of more than thirty minutes. People are not so forgiving in real life. Conflicts with your friends and other relationships won't resolve themselves easily. (Remember that "no scriptwriter" thing.) You will have to put effort into restoring broken relationships. Don't think that you're a bad person (or that your friends are) just because it takes longer than one episode to solve a problem. (On the other hand, don't let your life be like a soap opera by stretching the same argument over thirteen years.)

4. In real life, your conflicts won't end with a punch line. In the sitcoms, any problem can be solved with a great punch line. Well, not in real life. Your problems won't all be resolved in thirty minutes, and some broken relationships may not get fixed at all. There are going to be some people who won't ever be your friends because they just don't like you (yes, we know, it is very shortsighted of them). In real life, you're going to have to learn to live with people who are your enemies.

5. In real life, you don't always get the same table. Sitcom friendships don't require a lot of effort for "the gang" to get together. After all, they always manage to get the same table at the diner or the same couch at the coffeehouse. That's not going to happen with you and your friends (especially if you own the diner or coffee shop, because then you want paying customers sitting there instead of moochers who just use the place for posterior support).

In real life, you are going to have to work hard at building your relationships. It takes time and effort and creativity. Don't think that your relationships are sub-par just because you have to sit at a different table each time.

6. In real life, a lot happens outside of prime time. You wouldn't watch sitcoms if they were boring, so the directors always make sure that something funny and interesting is happening. That's why no one has ever considered using your life as the premise for a sitcom. (We are not saying that *you* are boring, but you'll have to admit that much of your life is filled with tedious, boring tasks.)

Don't be dissatisfied with your life and your relationships just because part of each day is spent in mundane routine. Hey, even the sitcom characters must have a boring life because their wacky adventures only happen for a half hour once a week.

7. In real life, you actually have to work at the office. While we are on the subject of boring routines and tedious tasks, let's talk about your job. People in sitcom life don't actually work very often or very hard. Hard work isn't funny. But an incompetent boss is funny, so every sitcom job has one. Your boss may be incompetent, too, but that probably isn't very funny in your situation.

In real life, your boss isn't going to let you goof off like the characters in the sitcoms. You can get fired if you aren't productive. And the very least, you'll have a lot more tension and a lot less frivolity at your job. Get used to it. That's why they call it "work." If you're anxious to have wacky adventures, you'll have to have them after work. We suggest Thursday nights.

8. In real life, it's not all about sex. We are two guys who have each been married to our wives for a bunch of years. We each married our college sweetheart. Neither of us messed around before marriage, and we haven't messed around since (except with our own wives). So, you might think that we don't know much about sex.

Well, we don't know anything about sitcom sex, and we never want to—and neither should you. Sitcoms put an emphasis on sex that far exceeds any semblance of real life. Contrary to what you see on television, it is actually possible to have conversations without double entendre. And it is actually possible to have a meaningful relationship with a person of the opposite sex that is predicated on more than physical urges and raging hormones.

9. In real life, the "extras" have feelings, too. There are always a lot of people in the scenes of sitcoms who never speak. You see them sitting at the nearby restaurant table or on the next seat in the subway, moving their mouths—but no sound ever emanates from their oral orifice. These people never talk because the producers would have to pay them more money. These "extras" are irrelevant to the storyline.

As we will be discussing in Part II, you have a lot of people in the scenes of your life, but none of them are irrelevant extras. They each have feelings and emotions. You should pay attention to some of these individuals. Get to know them. Let them talk. You may be enriched by what they have to say (and you won't have to pay them a cent more if you let them speak).

10. In real life, outtakes don't get edited. In sitcoms, the flubs magically disappear. The directors cut out the mistakes (and then sell them to Dick Clark for those insipid "Blooper" shows). However, *your* mistakes don't get edited out of real life. You've got to watch what you say and how you act because you can't take it back. Dick Clark is not interested in your bloopers because everyone will have already seen or heard about them—and they will be remembered for a long time. This means that success in your relationships will require thoughtfulness (or at least a brain that can process your thoughts faster than your mouth repeats them).

If You Have Been Deprogrammed, You're Ready to Connect

You can't accurately analyze your life and your relationships if your expectations are derived from the fallacies and fantasies that you'll see on TV. But if you are able to delete these erroneous images from your mind, then we offer you our hearty "congratulations" and we implore you to keep reading. Now you're ready to connect. And that's what your life is all about: connections.

CHAPTER 3

Created to Connect

Movies and television sitcoms aside, everybody is connected to everybody else these days. Never before have we had so many devices and programs that give us the ability to access information (useful and trivial), entertainment (good and bad), and other people (friends and strangers)—all at the same time!

The whole world is wired. In any given day you will use fiber optics, cable, satellites, antennae, cellular sites, and good old-fashioned snail mail so you can communicate with something or someone else.

When you think about all of these connections going on each and every day, it's a little bewildering. What is everybody doing? Well, we don't have any reliable

Factoid

Each day in America there are ...
200 million Internet connections
100 million E-mail messages
50 million phone calls
25 million letters
... and that doesn't count the millions who go to the movies, watch television, and listen to the radio!

statistics to back us up, but here's what we think is happening:

- *E-trading.* The popularity of such Web sites as eBay and E*Trade is on the rise. We estimate that at any given moment, 63 percent of all people are buying or selling stuff.
- *E-normous time wasting:* Based on our own experience, we guess that 35 percent of all people are either sending or receiving useless jokes and urban legends via E-mail.
- *rE-turning:* 26 percent of all people are trying to return stuff they purchased over the Internet.
- *Reach out and smack someone:* Simply by observing people while driving, we estimate that 22 percent of all people are on cell phones making calls to other people on cell phones at any given moment. Compare that to the 3 percent of people who call their mothers in a given week, unless it's Mother's Day!
- *Pull the plug:* 18 percent of all people are watching reruns of TV sitcoms on any given night. The other 82 percent are watching shows with the words "Judge," "Cops," or "Millionaire" in the title.

OK, so maybe our research methods are a little suspect, but our point is this: everybody is connected, but few people are really *connecting*. You read that right. Just because you are connected through a Web site, satellite, or cellulite, it doesn't mean you are meaningfully linked to another person.

When you really *connect* with someone, you don't merely exchange information or conduct a transaction. When you connect, you *join together* with another person, whether you do it physically, emotionally, mentally, or spiritually. True connections are—

- *Personal:* Disembodied voices, disinterested order takers, and electronic devices do not count. A personal encounter is one with a living, breathing human being who is willing to exchange real names (first *and* last). You should at least be able to engage in a two-way, personal conversation.
- *Intimate:* We're not talking about you-know-what (and even that isn't very intimate for many people). True intimacy between people occurs when they know each other very well. Two or more people can be intimate when they know the personalities and personal preferences of a

person or people. In other words, intimacy occurs between close friends.

- *Satisfying:* Truly connecting with someone is a very satisfying experience (by contrast, casual connections are usually very frustrating). Something in you is completed, because you know—and you are known by—at least one other person.

Bruce & Stan's First Law of Relationships

As we are writing this book, there are two things that amaze us. The first is the incredible array of technology that makes it possible for just about anyone on earth to connect with just about anyone else, instantly and with very little effort. We can pick up a wireless device the size of a Twinkie, and in less than a minute be connected to virtually any other person on the globe. We can go to the Internet, type in "parakeet," and within seconds have access to more information than we would ever need about a truly useless bird. The technology that connects us with information and ideas is amazing, something that until recently was considered nothing more than science fiction.

The second thing that amazes us is that you are actually reading this book, which depends on a technology developed more than five and a half centuries ago. Books are produced today utilizing pretty much the same technology that Johannes Gutenberg used to build the first commercial printing press in 1455. The reason you use this rather antiquated form of communication is that these pages somehow give you a "warmer" feeling of connection than some computer device. As a result, you feel more connected to us (and we to you), even though we've never met.

From these two observations, we have developed a little theory based on the advancement of technology throughout history and its relationship to the need of humans to truly connect. Here it is:

Bruce & Stan's First Law of Relationships

The more technology advances, the more we become isolated from one another. And the more isolated we become, the greater our desire grows to truly connect.

To help explain Bruce & Stan's First Law of Relationships, we've come up with some examples of technological advancements in human history. Next to each technology we tell you what it did to disconnect people, and then what people came up with to better connect with each other.

Technological Advance	Immediate Impact	Eventual Result
Fire is discovered.	Family members could venture out at night.	The tradition of telling stories around the campfire was started, keeping the family home most nights.
The wheel is invented.	Transportation to places outside the cave was now possible, even if you had to use the family ox.	First Tupperware parties were started (of course, the first containers were made of rock).
Roads are developed.	Now you could travel many miles from your home in search of greater opportunity.	First family reunions were organized. Also, first time the question, "Could you bring a casserole?" was ever asked.
The printing press is invented by Gutenberg.	People no longer depended on the family campfire for stories and information.	First book clubs were organized (the most popular being the "Johanne's Picks Club," because Gutenberg was the only guy who knew how to read).
The Pony Express first appears.	For the first time, people could mail messages to one another instead of talking face to face.	Dick Clark became the spokesman for the world's first Publisher's Clearinghouse contest.
The telephone is invented.	As a result, people could call each other rather than write letters.	The first telemarketers appeared, which at first didn't bring people together, but it did get people talking about how much they hated telemarketers.
Personal computers are developed.	As a result, people could connect through E-mail and the Internet without ever leaving their homes.	We predict a revival of the tradition of telling stories around the campfire in an effort to "connect" again.

Yearning to Connect

History teaches us that every advance in technology has led to a greater desire to truly connect (which is the crux of Bruce & Stan's First Law of Relationships). And if that's the case, then our desire must be very great, because the technology we have at our disposal right now is pretty advanced (and yes, we know, it's only going to get more advanced).

How great is the desire right now? Ah, we thought you'd never ask. Allow us to take you to San Jose, California, in the heart of Silicon Valley, arguably the technological center of the universe. There are more very smart people in Silicon Valley, devoted to developing faster and more realistic connections, than anywhere else on earth. Hundreds of high-tech companies employ tens of thousands of high-tech workers, just so the rest of us can better connect with the world (and engage in endless hours of useless video entertainment).

Is there anything happening in this human laboratory that confirms Bruce & Stan's First Law of Relationships? Absolutely. Check out this headline and excerpt of an extensive article by Janice Rombeck in the *San Jose Mercury News* on the condition of people working in the high-tech industry:

On-the-Job Communities

"In a region known for demanding work schedules and two-job families struggling to keep up with housing costs, homes across Silicon Valley often are empty from dawn until after dark. But many residents still strive to connect with their neighbors and communities. Despite their hard work, Silicon Valley residents make time to form communities with others who share their interests. People come together at schools, clubs, and churches."

For those Silicon Valley workers who spend "far more waking hours at their workplace than at home," communities have begun to flourish on the job. At least one church sponsors groups of high-tech workers at small weekly gatherings, and more such groups are expected to spring up. As high-tech workers face increasing pressure to make the workplace "their all-consuming life," many people "yearn for spiritual meaning and a richer sense of community" (more about "Working Together" in Chapter 8).

Does any of this sound familiar?

Biblical Connections

This yearning for spiritual meaning and a richer sense of community isn't lim-ited to high-tech workers in Silicon Valley. We have the same yearning, and so do you. This isn't a psychological weakness or some kind of touchy-feely movement that will eventually die out. This yearning burns in the heart and soul of every human being—put there by the Creator of the universe. We can't help needing to connect on a deep and meaningful level—that's the way God made us.

Connected to Our Creator

God didn't create us so we could wander around aimlessly, finding meaning only in the material things of this world. He created us to be in relationship with him. Beginning with Adam and Eve, God literally stamped his image in our very beings (see Genesis 1:27).

You know that connection you have with your biological parents? It's there, and there's nothing you can do to change it (although you'd like to sometimes). Whether you like it or not, you resemble and imitate your par-ents in many ways.

It's no different for God and us. We resemble our Creator—not in the physical sense, but in the spiritual dimension of our lives. The connection is there whether we admit it or not. King Solomon, considered the wisest man who ever lived, put it this way: "God has ... planted eternity in the human heart" (Ecclesiastes 3:11).

You have made us for yourself, and our hearts are restless till they find their rest in you.

St. Augustine

The apostle Paul wrote that even people who refuse to acknowledge God (who "push truth away from themselves") know in their heart of hearts the truth of God's existence. Why? Because "God has put this knowledge in their hearts" (Romans 1:18-19). So the first and most basic need of every human being is to connect with God.

Connected to Each Other

After the need to connect with God comes our need to connect with each other. Once again, that's the way God made us.

> No man is an Island, entire of itself, every man
> is a piece of the Continent, a part of the main.
>
> John Donne

Let's take a look at some of these human connections, using the Bible as our guide. The Bible is more than a book of thee's and thou's and do's and don'ts; it is God's personal message to us (that's why they sometimes call it "God's Word"). The Bible contains everything we need for living and connecting, because it was written by God, who made us and knows everything about us (see Hebrews 4:12).

If you want to know about relationships, study the Bible. To get you started, we're going to highlight five different relationships you are likely to encounter in your lifetime. Since we're going to devote full chapters to each of these relationships later in the book, we're not going to go into a lot of detail in this chapter. But we do want to give you an overview so you can see for yourself that relationships are God's idea. And no matter how hard we try to disconnect the relationships, we won't be happy until we connect with each other in these different ways.

- *The relationship between men and women.* This is the most basic and potentially the most intimate of all human relationships. The greatest expression of human love and companionship takes place between a man and a woman. Why? Because that's the way God created us.

Check out Genesis 2:18-25. There you'll find that God made Adam first. God said: "It is not good for the man to be alone. I will make a companion who will help him" (Genesis 2:18). So God made Eve from Adam's own body to be the perfect complement to his maleness. When God brought Eve to Adam, here's how the Bible describes Adam's rather enthusiastic reaction: "At last!" Adam exclaimed. "She is part of my own flesh and bone! She will be called 'woman' because she was taken out of man" (Genesis 2:23). In the very next verse we learn that God designed marriage to be the ultimate relationship between a man and a woman (more about that in Chapter 7).

"Marriage Isn't the Ultimate Relationship"

Does every person need to get married in order to enjoy the ultimate male-female relationship? Well, yes and no. *Yes*, you need to get married in order to enjoy the ultimate *male-female* relationship as God designed it; but *no*, you don't need to get married in order to enjoy the ultimate relationship, which is between humans and God. In fact, married people can't experience the depths of their relationship with God in the same way unmarried people can. The apostle Paul wrote that single people who maintain their purity can serve God more effectively than married people, who must think about their "earthly responsibilities," including how to please their husband or wife (1 Corinthians 7:32-34).

• *Family.* It didn't take long from the time the first humans were created for a population explosion to occur. The Bible says that "the human population began to grow rapidly on the earth" (Genesis 6:1). The Bible also tells us that before long, things weren't going real well. To put it bluntly, people were rotten through and through (Bible word: *wicked*). God saw that "all their thoughts were consistently and totally evil. So the Lord was sorry he had ever made them. It broke his heart" (Genesis 6:5-6).

You know the story. Our loving Creator was so heartbroken that he decided to wipe out the human race and every other living thing. It was almost the end of the world, except for one man—Noah. We can thank God that there was at least one righteous man on the earth who "found favor with God," because "he consistently followed God's will and enjoyed a close relationship with him" (Genesis 6:9). So God spared Noah and his family from destruction. They were saved by God's grace.

Noah and the flood was a literal event, but the story has a spiritual application for you and your family. First, your defiance against God or your faithfulness to him doesn't affect just you. Its effect extends to your family as well, for bad or for good. Second, God loves families and will protect them from the evil influences of the world—if we follow his will and enjoy a close relationship with him (more about families in Chapter 5).

- *Enemies.* There are many examples of how God has preserved the family. One great story is found later in the Book of Genesis, when Joseph (the proud owner of the Technicolor dream coat) was sold into slavery by his brothers, who in effect became his enemies. Even though nobody knew it at the time, God was working to preserve the family.

By God's grace, Joseph went from Egyptian slave to high-ranking official. Meanwhile, his father, Jacob, and his siblings were suffering through a famine in Israel. Because of his position, Joseph was able to bring his family—including the brothers who once were his enemies—to Egypt and literally save their lives. In a classic statement that applies to all enemies, Joseph told his brothers, "As far as I am concerned, God turned into good what you meant for evil" (Genesis 50:20). For more on enemies and difficult people, see Chapter 9.

- *Friends.* Friendship is God's idea. He created us to be his friends, and he loves it when we form deep and meaningful friendships with others. The best example of friendship in the Bible is found in the story of Jonathan and David. It's a classic story of love, loyalty, forgiveness, and sacrifice—the qualities that make true friendships what they are.

Jonathan was King Saul's son, and David was King Saul's enemy (mainly because David was designated by God to be the next king). At the risk of offending his father, Jonathan saved David's life (read all about it in 1 Samuel 20). Jonathan made a vow of friendship with David, "for Jonathan loved David as much as he loved himself" (1 Samuel 20:17).

Jonathan and David's friendship was more than skin-deep. It was a spiritual connection rooted in God, who wants very much to be our friend (for more on friendships, see Chapter 6).

• *Community.* We normally think of a "community" as a place where people live, such as a district or town. But in the best sense of the word, a community is made up of people who share something in common.

A college is a community because everyone there is studying a particular field of knowledge (OK, almost everyone). People who share a particular interest are a community as well. No doubt you've heard of someone being a member of the "arts community."

The highest form of community is spiritual, because it involves people connected together by their interest in knowing God better. In his book *The Safest Place on Earth*, Dr. Larry Crabb writes: "The church is a community of people on a journey to God." By *church* he doesn't necessarily mean the First Baptist Church on the corner of Third and Main, and neither does God. The Bible says that the church includes all who have put their faith in God (see 1 Corinthians 12:13). Another way to describe church is "spiritual community."

Dr. Crabb suggests that when people connect in a spiritual community, they are on the road to authenticity and the true meaning of life (more about the meaning of life in Chapter 12).

The Greatest Connection of All

We began this chapter by talking about how we can instantly connect with virtually anyone or anything on the planet. We concluded that our ability to connect doesn't necessarily mean we are truly connecting with others in a way that is personal, intimate, and satisfying. In fact, the more technology enables us to connect, the less connected we feel.

There's no question that people everywhere yearn for spiritual meaning and a richer sense of community. It doesn't matter who you are or where you are in life. Sooner or later you are going to realize that any kind of connection you make with others is going to go flat (kind of like that open Pepsi can in your fridge) unless you invite God into the mix. If God isn't in your life and your relationships—no matter how intimate or how casual they are—here's what's going to happen:

- You're going to base your relationships on what people can do for you, not the other way around.
- You will have a tendency to control rather than encourage people.
- Since you don't have a reference point for truth outside of yourself (i.e., God), you will inevitably use yourself as the reference point for truth, and that will change according to the situation. The results of your *performance* will be more important to you than the truth of your *position*.
- When you experience difficulties and pain, you will have no one to turn to but yourself.
- Without a spiritual dimension to your life, the material dimension is all you have. And when the material stuff is gone (including you), that's all there is. Game over, man.

On the other hand, if God is in your life and your relationships—no matter how intimate or how casual they are—then here's what's going to happen:

- You're going to base your relationships on what you can do for others, not the other way around.
- You will want to encourage people rather than control them.
- With God and his Word as your reference point, you will always have a standard for truth.
- When you experience difficulties and pain, you can turn to God, who promises to help you.
- Because your life has a spiritual dimension, you have something eternal to look forward to after all the temporary material stuff (including your body) is gone.

This is where you make the greatest connection of all.

Turning Maslow Inside Out
In Abraham Maslow's "hierarchy of needs" (Chapter 1), you start with the

most basic needs of food, shelter, and clothing—then move up to security, love, esteem, and self-actualization.

When you leave God out of your life and relationships, your constant goal is to reach the top of Abe's hierarchy, where you hope to find meaning in yourself. All of your connections are meaningful only as they help you "actu-alize" yourself. This is why popular psychologists, talk show hosts, and writ-ers will tell you to find meaning in your inner "spirit" (and they're not talk-ing about the Holy Spirit). When God isn't in the process, all you have is *you.*

When God is in your life and your relationships, Abe's little ladder of needs gets turned inside out. With God in the mix, you can trust him for your basic physical needs (see Matthew 6:31-33). On the other end of the spectrum, God meets your esteem needs and your hunger for significance. That leaves the middle part of the hierarchy—the part with the need to love and be loved—as the main concern. And here's where you need to spend most of your time.

No one loves you more than your Creator (see 1 John 4:9-10), and because he loves you so much, you have the capacity to love others. In fact, you are commanded to love others (Matthew 22:39), which is the basis for designing and building your relationship network.

"God's Hierarchy"

When we were growing up, we learned a little acrostic for the word "Joy" that summarized what we're talking about here. The idea was that if you want real joy in your life, you have to put your connections in this order:

J: If you want to connect with God, you must first connect with Jesus, who came to earth to make us right with God (see Romans 3:25).
O: After you have a relationship with God through Jesus, you will want to connect with others. Jesus said that after loving God with all heart, soul, and mind you should love your neighbor (see Matthew 22:37-39).
Y: Finally, there's you. You need to connect with yourself and love your-self, but only after you have connected with God and other people (see Matthew 22:39).

In the seven chapters of Part II, we're going to focus on your various connections—your family, your friends, that very special person in your life, your co-workers, the difficult people in your life, and your neighbors. Rather than letting these relationships happen "on their own," we're going to encourage you to proactively design your relationship network.

Part II

Your Real Life
and Your Network

Three men are my friends. He that loves me, he that hates me, and he that is indifferent to me. He who loves me teaches me tenderness. He who hates me teaches me caution. He who is indifferent to me teaches me self-reliance.

Parin

CHAPTER 4

Designing Your
Relationship Network

With how many people did you connect today? Probably hundreds. Think about the people you encountered from the time you got up this morning:

- Maybe you grunted at a roommate or two as you stumbled out of bed on your way to the bathroom or refrigerator early this morning.
- Then there were those people you snubbed in the elevator of your condo on the way to the parking garage.
- Next, there was the "cashier girl" at the Java Jungle drive-thru who makes your daily latte supplement.
- Don't forget the several drivers on the freeway who waved at you (with one digit prominently displayed) when you swerved after spilling the latte in your lap.
- The "toll booth lady," who looks a lot like the "lunchroom lady" from your high school, only without the mole.
- And from the downtown parking lot to your office desk: "parking lot attendant guy"; the bustling hordes you bumped on the sidewalk; the

homeless person you stepped over at the newspaper stand; more zombies snubbed in the elevator; Diana, the annoying receptionist; and the "juice-and-muffin cart guy" who sold you a Danish and made some remark about the big brown wet spot on your pants that you couldn't quite hide with your briefcase.

And all of those were before 9:05 A.M. Throughout the rest of the day, you had more connections with people in meetings, on the phone, via E-mail, and by correspondence. You made about as many connections driving home as you did in the morning commute (except no one waved at you). By the end of the day, you have connected with more people than the greeter at Wal-Mart.

Let's face it. Our lives are filled with lots of other people. Every day you are going to be connecting with multitudes of people unless:

- You have a home office and eat only Domino's pizza delivered to your door.
- You live in a Biosphere.
- You are involved with one of those promotional e-commerce projects in which you live in a house with three strangers and have to order everything off the Internet.

We'll assume that you don't fall into any of these categories (although we're sure the pizza delivery option has some appeal to you). Not all of the contacts you make will seem important at first. They will fall into various categories of significance. Some will be:

- *Inconsequential:* When you greet some stranger you pass in the lobby of your office building.
- *Monumental:* When the new person moving into your apartment building later becomes your best friend, and you start a software company together that makes you rich after the IPO (initial public stock offering).
- *Accidental:* When you rear-end a car because you weren't paying attention to where you were driving.
- *Intentional:* When you rear-end another car *on purpose* because it was the only way you could get the name and telephone number of the attractive driver.

- *Regrettable:* When that attractive driver turns out to be married to the city's premier personal-injury lawyer.

Most of your contacts will happen randomly, without plan or purpose. But it doesn't have to be that way. In fact, it shouldn't be that way. The contacts that are dictated by your circumstances can affect what happens to you, but the relationships that are determined by your choices usually affect who you become. So ...

You should be proactively engaged in efforts to establish and develop relationships that are determined by choice, not dictated by circumstance.

In this chapter we'll discuss the benefits of being deliberate about your relationships. We're going to go over some of the same topics we covered in Part I, and we're going to preview some of the same topics we'll be covering throughout Part II. Our purpose in this chapter is to categorize them differently in the hope that, one way or another, you will understand what we're trying to say.

What's God Got to Do With It?

In Chapter 3, we talked about how God created you to connect—first with him, and then with others. But if God is so big on this "connection" thing, shouldn't we just sit back and let him manipulate the circumstances of our lives until he links us up with the people we are supposed to meet? That's a fair question, but it doesn't take a monk in a monastery to answer it.

Yes, God wants us to connect with other people. And, yes, God is sovereign (nothing happens without his knowledge and permission), and he can control and direct all of the events of the universe if he chooses to do so. But he also gave each of us a free will and a brain (some more, some less). He wants us to make intelligent choices about the people with whom we establish relationships.

Situational Acquaintances

Dr. Norm Wright says that most people are in "situations" rather than "relationships." We agree. Most people connect with a lot of people, but they haven't made the affirmative choice to build a relationship with any of them. Instead, they allow the situations and circumstances of life to dictate the dynamics of their connection to each other. Here are a few examples of the types of "situational acquaintances" that you might have in your life:

Your Family

Your familial unit is perhaps the prime example of people that you are involved with (notice that we delicately refrained from saying "stuck with") because of circumstances instead of choice. The circumstances of your birth, not the exercise of your choice, impacts:

- **Who You Are:** You had no opportunity to choose your parents, but you got their images stamped all over your DNA. We know that you haven't complained to us about Claude and Maude, but we know that you fantasize how life could be different if there had been a few professional athletes, super models, geniuses, and Wall Street gurus swimming in your family's gene pool.
- **What You Do:** It really isn't your choice to spend every Thanksgiving with the relatives at Granny's house in Pasadena (forcing you to decline a ski trip to Aspen with the gang from work). And it seems like the best weekends of the year are spent at weddings of relatives you hardly know (and sometimes wish you didn't). But you do these things anyway. Why? Because you are part of the family. Choice has nothing to do with it—unfortunately for you.

We aren't saying that your family is a bunch of losers. But you might feel that way if you abandon all hope of meaningful friendships outside Maude, Claude, and the rest of the kinfolk. But don't despair. It is possible to have meaningful relationships with family members. In Chapter 5 we will show you that your family members can have much more significance to you than being potential kidney transplant donors.

Your Neighbors

Even when you escape family gatherings and return to your own home, you are surrounded by more "situational acquaintances." The neighbors who live beside you are there because of circumstances and not by your choice. Whether you are living in a dorm, in an apartment, or in a house on a cul-de-sac, you've got neighbors who lived there before you or moved in afterward, and nobody asked your opinion or permission.

You don't even know some of your neighbors (except you exchange nods of the head when you see each other taking out the garbage). Others you may know casually (having exchanged opinions about the weather, sports, and restaurants—staying away from controversial topics like politics, religion, or anything involving feelings or emotions). A few of your neighbors may be your close friends (you know, like the typical "across-the-hall neighbors" in those sitcoms—neighbors who barge in unannounced, forage through your refrigerator, and inquire about the intimacies of your personal life).

As you analyze your life and your relationships, here are a few tips for dealing with the neighbors who have found their way into your life:

- *Neighbor Tip #1: Be friendly to each of your neighbors.* Just because these neighbors were thrust upon you without your consent is no excuse to be rude. You shouldn't even be indifferent. In fact, try to extend a little courtesy to each of them. You'll feel better about yourself if you are pleasant to your neighbors. (Hey, if he goes berserk and starts slashing tires and breaking windows, you want him to skip your car because he remembers that you brought him chicken soup when he had the sniffles.)

- *Neighbor Tip #2: Your neighbor doesn't have to be your best friend.* Don't feel obligated to adopt your neighbor as your best friend. It's enough to be friendly (see Neighbor Tip #1). If you move your neighbor into the "best friend" category out of guilt, it will be an unfulfilling relationship for both of you. Take a lesson from the United States and Canada. We Americans are polite and friendly to our neighbors to the North, but we don't invite Canadians over to dinner every night.

- *Neighbor Tip #3: Best friends don't always make good neighbors, but it is great when your neighbor becomes your best friend.* You can ruin a good friendship by becoming neighbors (or housemates) with your friend. All of your friend's little idiosyncrasies that never bothered you before will be amplified when they are living a few feet away from you. They'll soon become major annoyances, and your friendship is likely to be jeopardized. It is much better when you simply start out being friendly to the neighbors that you've got (see Neighbor Tip #1) and you let that friendship build without any pressure to be best friends (see Neighbor Tip #2), and each of you are drawn to a deeper friendship with each other for meaningful reasons (other than you share the same carport).

In Chapter 10 we'll talk about how to develop meaningful relationships with your neighbors.

Your Co-Workers

The people who work in your office are much like your neighbors at home. Think about it:

- They were there when you moved into your cubicle, or they arrived after you did.
- You didn't have any choice in the matter. (Your boss made the decision.)
- You spend a large portion of your life just a few feet away from them.
- You get together occasionally for "block parties" (held in the employees' break room).
- You can exchange opinions about the weather, sports, and restaurants— but you stay away from controversial topics like politics, religion, or anything involving feelings or emotions.

Basically, the same friendship rules for neighbors apply to your co-workers. You ought to be nice to them (make this Co-Worker Tip #1), but you shouldn't feel obligated to turn them into your best friends just because you share the same restroom and you have matching company shirts (you guessed it, Co-Worker Tip #2).

Unfortunately, many of your co-workers don't have a copy of this book, so they are deprived of our insightful insights into the dynamics of situational acquaintances of the occupational variety. So, they might be expecting that you are going to be best friends with each other. After all, you have been nice to them, so they just assumed that you wanted to be best friends (which is a drawback of Co-Worker Tip #1). If this happens, you need to be prepared for the barrage of invitations that involve increasing intimacy:

Stage 1:   Invitations to eat lunch together every day.

Stage 2:   Invitations to stop off at the corner Starbucks after work each night.

Stage 3:   Invitations to spend your weekends at the Star Trek conventions (wearing the obligatory Klingon costume).

Now, you might not mind Stage 1 because you have to eat lunch anyway; and Stage 2 isn't so bad because you like to give the parking garage thirty minutes to clear out; but Stage 3 involves a commitment that you may be hesitant to make (because no one looks good as a Klingon or in those tight polyester Star Trek shirts). You have to draw the line somewhere.

The challenge with office friendships is to appear friendly without misleading people who are lonely and in search of a best friend. In other words, you need to learn to be courteous without being sucked into Stage 3. There is a balance in all of this. You don't have to totally avoid Stages 1 and 2. In fact, lunch with a co-worker and after-hours socializing may be enjoyable for you. And common courtesy, civility, and Christianity should prompt you to an occasional act of kindness. (Who knows, in a wave of euphoria you might even volunteer to help someone move furniture to a new apartment over the weekend.) But as these relationships develop, you might want to do some advance planning so you'll be able to decline the Stage 3 invitations without hurting anyone's feelings.

The trick is to come up with a plausible excuse that will dissuade your co-workers from extending a Stage 3 invitation to you ever again. You might try something like this:

> Thanks for the invitation. I'm supposed to go to my Multiple Personality Disorder therapy group, but I'm sure I'll be OK if I miss this session. I'll be there. Please reserve a table of six for me.

Don't expect that the person in the next cubicle is going to be your best friend. It's not likely to happen. After all, you were just thrown together by the whim of your boss (and because your company was too cheap to give you a private office). We'll talk more about building relationships with your co-workers in Chapter 8. For now, we just want you to realize that meaningful friendships require more than a mutual dislike of the boss and matching desk sets.

Intentional Relationships

We hope the people in your *situational* relationships—your family, neighbors, and co-workers—provide you with meaningful relationships in your life. That is our hope, but it may not be a reasonable expectation. These people who are thrown into your life by circumstance may not have the character and qualities that are necessary for a deep friendship. As a result, your life might seem a little empty if your contacts are limited to the people you will find at the family reunion, or the people you meet at the apartment trash receptacle, or the people standing around the office photocopy machine.

If your life seems to be lacking fulfilling friendships, don't despair. Your situational acquaintances won't occupy all the time and energy in your life (unless you let them). You can take an affirmative step toward establishing connections with the type of people that your life presently lacks. We call these people *intentional* relationships, and we call the process "designing your relationship network." Simply put, here is how it works:

> **Rather than letting your circumstances dictate your best friendships, use some affirmative steps to establish relationships with people who can bring meaning and significance to your life.**

Let us give you a few examples of the types of people you may wish to bring into your life by choice.

God. We've already talked about the importance of connecting with God, but we want to mention it again in the context of making your relationship with God intentional. You might think that God is a situational acquaintance: He brought you into this world, and he's always hanging around, whether you're interested in him or not. In that sense, God is a situational acquaintance, but we are suggesting that you make him much more than that.

We think you should take some affirmative steps to develop an intimate, personal relationship with God. He may be hanging around, but God won't force himself on you. He is the perfect gentleman. He waits for you to come to him. In fact, he is hanging around just so he will be there immediately whenever you decide you want to know him better.

In the Old Testament, God explained this principle to the Hebrew nation:

If you look for me in earnest, you will find me when you seek me.

JEREMIAH 29:13

In the New Testament, the same principle is presented to all of the people of the world:

Look! Here I stand at the door and knock. If you hear me calling and open the door, I will come in, and we will share a meal as friends.

REVELATION 3:20

In Chapter 12 we'll talk in more detail about developing a relationship with God. For now, we just want you to consider that part of any emptiness in your life might be a spiritual dimension that can only be filled by God. Put him on your "intentional relationships" list.

Mentors

Mentoring is the process where a wise individual (the mentor) nurtures and encourages the personal development of someone else (the protégé). The relationship can be centered on something specific (such as career advice) or life in general.

Mentoring became a lost art in the final decades of the twentieth century. The "Me Generation" of the 1970s had a slogan: "Don't trust anyone over thirty." Well, that really cut down on the mentor pool. The only people left weren't too interested in being mentors (love beads and peace-sign necklaces are a distraction to any serious mentoring relationship). Twenty years later, when the hippies of the seventies were running the big corporations that they had protested against, they didn't know how to be mentors because they had never had mentors. So, the young adults of the nineties were deprived of the advice and insight of mentors as well (even though it was then socially acceptable to trust people over the age of thirty—provided they weren't still wearing love beads and a peace-sign necklace).

Just when we thought mentoring was gone and forgotten, a TV show and a book brought mentoring back into vogue:

- On an episode of "Seinfeld," several characters were involved in mentoring situations. Of course, the portrayal of the mentor relationship was a bit skewed (although it made for some good laughs), but the terminology of "mentor" and "protégé" was reintroduced into the vernacular.

- Without ever mentioning mentorship, the best-selling book *Tuesdays With Morrie* provided an excellent example of how the relationship works. This book told the true story of a journalist who learned that his former coach was dying of cancer. Regular visits to Morrie turned out to be lessons about what is important in life. (Note: Don't find an old person to be your mentor just so you can write a best-selling book. It's already been done.)

If you are serious about being intentional about your relationship network, you need to consider who might be a mentor to you. Here are a few pointers to help get you started:

1. You have to approach potential mentors; they won't come looking for you. Good mentors are those who are succeeding already in the area in which you wish to get their advice. They won't be interested in wasting their time if you aren't serious (besides, they've read *Tuesdays With Morrie*, and they know what happens at the end.)

2. Beware of people who beg to be your mentor. It might be an indication that they are more interested in elevating their own image than in helping you.

3. Be willing to commit to a regular schedule. Mentoring doesn't work well if you connect with your mentor only when you feel an urge to do so. (Urges are poor indicators of just about everything except gastrointestinal disorders.) Part of the benefit of having a mentor is the discipline it brings to your life.

4. Be willing to change the schedule to accommodate your mentor. The mentor is doing *you* a favor, so you need to give the mentor latitude to rearrange the meeting if a conflict arises in the mentor's schedule. (Most mentors take their role very seriously and give it a high priority, so we don't think that you'll have to change the schedule very often.)

5. Be prepared with meaningful questions. The mentor will want to give you advice that is relevant to your situation, so you'll have to ask questions to indicate the issues that you are struggling with.

6. Don't blindly follow the mentor's advice. Even though you appreciate (and need) the advice that your mentor offers, you still have the personal responsibility for determining whether the advice fits your own situation, your personality, and your beliefs. Receive the advice, but use it as it fits your own situation. (The best mentor generally will *not* be your immediate supervisor at work. Supervisors get upset if you don't obey their instructions. For the same reason, your mother is probably not the best mentor choice.)

7. Select a mentor whose chromosomes match yours. If you have two "x's," or an "x" and a "y" chromosome, then so should your mentor. In other words, avoid crossing gender lines. Gals need women mentors, and guys need mentors who are men. There is a strong relational bond that develops between a mentor and the protégé, and you don't want that relationship to have an appearance of being inappropriate.

You won't always be able to have a mentor. Your circumstances may not always permit it, and you might not always be able to find a mentor candidate. But seize the opportunity whenever it is available.

Your relationship with a mentor can be of a limited duration, but what you learn can benefit you for a lifetime.

Your Friends

Now we may be getting to the real reason that you bought this book. Establishing meaningful friendships perhaps will be your most difficult task as you design your relationship network. Why? Well, there are several reasons:

- We are tempted to let our friendships develop by circumstances rather than choice;
- A person's character isn't the first thing that you notice, and it takes a while for it to be revealed; and
- Most people don't know what it takes to be a good friend (or aren't prepared to give it).

In Chapter 6 we are going to explore in depth the subject of friendships. We'll analyze the character traits that make for a true friend. We think you'll agree that meaningful friendships—the *best friends* type—don't come easily and they don't come often. But we also think you'll agree that those meaningful friendships are worth every bit of the effort and are a very necessary component of your relationship network.

It may be a while until you get to Chapter 6, and you shouldn't have to wait that long to learn one of the key factors to building lasting friendships. And since some of this stuff is so good that we can't wait, we'll give you an important insight right now:

**A man that hath friends
must show himself friendly.**

We didn't make that up ourselves. It comes from Proverbs 18:24 in the King James Version of the Bible. (King James was much more inclined to use words like "hath" than we are.) Go ahead and think about that verse for a while. We'll talk to you about it more when we get to Chapter 6.

A Spouse

If you are going to be intentional about anyone in your relationship network, make it the person who is going to be your lifetime marriage partner. We aren't talking about designing intentional schemes and strategies that you will implement to trick this person into marrying you. We're talking about being intentional about:

- *The places where you will be looking for potential spouse candidates.* For example, are you more interested in finding a spouse who would hang out at a church group or a biker bar?

- *Scrutinizing clues about the character of potential spouse candidates.* For instance, you may wish to disqualify candidates if the business card of a bail bondsman falls out of their wallet.

- *Setting limits on the activities you'll participate in with potential spouse candidates.* Try to visualize how the activity will turn out before you agree to participate. If the conclusion you forecast involves hospitals, headlines, or prison, then decline the invitation. This person is not good marriage material.

- *Setting the standards you are looking for in a potential spouse candidate.* We think a list is helpful. But leave the clipboard at home on the first date.

In Chapter 7 we'll talk about whether marriage is right for you (because it is not for everyone). If you are thinking about taking that step toward the matrimonial aisle, then we'll give you a few pointers for making an intentional, well-informed decision *in advance* so you won't have any post-honeymoon regrets.

**Maybe you can't help falling in love,
but with a little planning you can determine
where you are going to fall.**

Unavoidable Encounters

You'll be glad that your *intentional* relationships are in your network, and usually you won't mind even the *situational* acquaintances that you come in contact with. But there is a third group that you would prefer to avoid. We refer to this third group as your *unavoidable* encounters.

You can't escape unavoidable encounters. (That's the reason they're called *unavoidable.*) You would like to, but you can't. However, your situation can be improved if you learn how to deal with them.

Difficult People

In the network of the people that you connect with, there are going to be a few that cause you great dermatological discomfort:

- They are a real irritation;
- They rub you the wrong way;
- They get under your skin; and
- They make your flesh crawl.

Unlike some rashes and other irritations, they won't vanish when you rub ointment on them (and doing so may create a whole new set of problems with them).

Sometimes you can simply rearrange the details of your life to avoid contact with these difficult people, but sometimes you can't. You're stuck for the duration if one of these difficult people is your boss, your mother-in-law, your neighbor, or your Siamese twin.

In Chapter 9 we'll give you some practical advice about dealing with difficult people. We can't make them improve, but with a little insight on how to relate with them, your life might get better (or at least your skin might clear up).

Satan

Don't bail on us now. We aren't going to get wacko on you. We aren't the kind of guys who think that you are demon-possessed every time you get the sniffles. And we don't think that there is a Satanic attack involved every time your car breaks down. (Those are just the natural results of walking outside to get the newspaper in your pajamas and bare feet, and of driving a 1984 Dodge Diplomat.) But Satan is very real, and he is very interested in your life.

Throughout this book we'll be talking about your relationship with God, and we'll be advising you to follow God's advice for dealing with the other people in your circle of contacts. But there's a downside to following God. The more you pay attention to God and what he says, the more Satan pays attention to you. One of the ways that Satan tries to mess up your life is through other people. He specializes in maximizing the damage from broken relationships, hurt feelings, enemies, and gossip.

In Chapter 12, we'll be talking in detail about your relationship with God. Part of our discussion will focus on the ways that you can defend yourself against Satan's interference in your life. You can't do it alone (our advice isn't *that* good); it will take God on your side to experience victory.

Let the Designing Begin

You wouldn't take a two-week European vacation without an itinerary. You wouldn't build a birdhouse without a plan. Most endeavors in life turn out so much better with a little advance planning. Developing your friendships and other relationships isn't any different. Your life will improve dramatically as you become more intentional about your relationship network.

Let's begin with the first group you were ever involved with: your family.

CHAPTER 5

It Begins With the Family

Question: What is it that connects you to every person in every culture from the beginning of time?

Answer: Family ("morning breath" is also acceptable).

Every person is part of a family. We all have a mother and a father, grandparents and cousins, great-grandparents and second cousins and so on. We all have an ancestry. Every person is a piece of fruit on the family tree. If we were to go back far enough, we would eventually end up with the same two first parents—Adam and Eve.

Family is what connects us all together. All of us came into the world through a family, and we have all been shaped into the people we are by family. You may love your family or resent your family or take it for granted. You may be the person who organizes your annual family reunion at the lake, or you could be on the verge of legally changing your name from sheer embarrassment. We don't know where you are with respect to your family. But there's one thing we do know—you can't disregard your family.

The Family Foundation

As you set out proactively to design and build your relationship network, think of it as your own personal construction project. With God as the architect of your life and your relationships, and the Bible as your blueprint, you have been given everything you need to succeed. Now it's up to you to put on your hard hat and get to work.

Every construction project starts with a foundation. The bigger the structure, the bigger the foundation. This is especially true of your relationship network. If you want to build it right and if you want to build it to last, you need a solid foundation, and that foundation has to be the family.

God and the Family

As you're going to see later in the chapter, God designed the family for a very specific purpose. In fact, God values the family so highly that he modeled his own relationship with us around the family structure.

Unless your family foundation is in place, all of your other relationships— your friends, your marriage partner, your co-workers, the difficult people in your life, and your neighbors—are going to be weaker. Oh, they may look good on the surface, but without a firm family foundation, your other relationships will have a tendency to crack and crumble under pressure.

Heritage and Legacy

There are two parts to this whole idea of family foundation: your *heritage* and your *legacy*.

- *Heritage:* This is your family background. You are a product of your family heritage, whether you like it or not. There's nothing you can do to change where you came from. You are either a proud progeny, with a glorious family history of heroes and achievers; or you are a victim of circumstances, with a family tree full of bad apples and lazy under-achievers; or you're like most of us—somewhere in between.

- *Legacy:* This is the part you *can* do something about, even if the story of your family heritage reads like a Stephen King novel. You may not have inherited a firm family foundation, but it is within your power to leave one behind.

Let's take a look at each of these parts of your overall family foundation, because each of them is vital to the success and the strength of your relationship network.

What Is Your Family DNA?

Before you can start a family foundation of your own, you have to figure out what kind of foundation you already have. The way you were raised and the environment in which you grew up have helped to shape the way you are today.

Let's approach this scientifically and discover the content of your family's *DNA*. That would be your family *Dynamic Range*, your family *Nurturing Quotient*, and your family *Activity Level* (OK, we admit it's a stretch, but stay with us).

- *Dynamic Range* – Every family has a way of operating, a certain style that's usually established by the head of the household. As you were growing up, what were the dynamics of your family?
  - *Dictatorship:* This family is directed by a strong, opinionated (loud?) parent whose motto is, "Do as I say, not as I do!" Some families don't take their dictator seriously (if he's the loveable type), but other families live in fear of their dictator (if he's the cranky type).
  - *Republic:* This kind of household is run by parents who let everyone in the family express opinions and desires before making decisions based on what they think is right. This is a "kinder, gentler" type of family, but the parents still make and enforce all the rules.
  - *Democracy:* The principle of "majority rules" characterizes the democratic family. There is still order in this family, but the kids may have as much say in running the household as the parents. Democratic families can be fun, but they can also be frustrating, since the

standards may shift according to the will of the people.

— *Laissez-Faire:* In this family, anything goes, because everyone pretty much does as he pleases. On the surface, this kind of situation sounds like a blast, but a laissez-faire family can breed insecurity in a kid, since you never really know where you stand.

— *Corporation:* The corporate family is run like a company. One parent acts as the family CEO, the other parent is the vice-president, and the kids are the frontline workers. Family assignments are "delegated" and performance is the ultimate measuring stick.

— *Relational:* This family is characterized by mutual respect and love. It's not that the other family styles lack these important family ingredients, but sometimes they are hidden behind the prevailing family dynamic. In this kind of family, relationships are more important than performance.

We want to make it clear that we aren't trying to pass judgment on which family dynamic is right or wrong. We aren't aware of any studies that show mass murderers come out of laissez-faire families, while child prodigies come from corporate families. The important thing for you to realize is that when it comes time for you to start your own family (should that time ever come), you are likely to adopt the same style of family dynamics you experienced as a child—unless you are determined to be different.

- *Nurturing Quotient :* This part of your family DNA has to do with the love you felt in your household. Any one of the families we just described is capable of expressing deep love and affection. Just because you came out of a dictatorship, for example, doesn't mean you didn't enjoy the benefits of a loving household. On the other hand, your family may have been very interactive, but it's possible that your parents rarely expressed love and affection for each other or for you. Think about the atmosphere in your home as you grew up. Were there expressions of love, or was it expected that you kept that stuff to yourself? You'd be surprised how much your family's nurturing quotient has molded you into the person you are today.

- *Activity Level :* Families are often characterized by their leisure activities. We know a father and son who race cars on weekends. Other families build their lives around soccer, while some enjoy ski weekends. You may have fond memories of camping in the mountains or at the beach with your family. Or how about that time your dad came home and announced, "We're going to Disney World," and he wasn't even the Super Bowl MVP? The types of activities your family enjoyed when you were growing up helped make you what you are today, and they will likely determine the kind of family you'll have in the future.

There's no ideal family DNA, just like there's no ideal genetic DNA. It's just the way your family is. But it's important to understand your background so you can better understand who you are.

The State of Your Family

Every year in January, the President of the United States gives the "State of the Union" address to a joint session of Congress. It's a big deal, with television cameras, a national audience, invited guests, and lots of enthusiastic applause.

Imagine that you have been chosen to deliver the "State of Your Family" address. It's going to be a big deal, with all of your immediate family members, some extended family, and a few invited guests in attendance. Everyone is anxious to hear what you're going to say about your family—the greatest family in the world. Keep in mind that you must be positive, but you must also be honest.

What areas in your family need improvement? What are you going to do—and what are you going to ask others in your family to do—to bring about these changes? What are the bright spots? What is your hope for the future?

You don't have to live at home to want to suggest ways for your family to improve. Even if you moved away from your family years ago, you still have that all-important family connection, and you still care about the way your family members relate to each other.

Use the space below to write out your "State of Your Family" speech (be sure to include dramatic pauses so your audience has time to applaud).

"Today's Family"

In their book *GenXers After God,* Todd Hahn and David Verhaagen write about "The Changing Family." They describe how the family has changed in the last few years because of our changing culture. See if any of these characteristics have affected your family's DNA:

The Fatherless Family – Your generation has the most "fatherless families" in our nation's history. As of 1998, 27 percent of all families were single-parent households, and 85 percent of these were without fathers. Even those families who have a father at home don't necessarily enjoy his full attention because of the next characteristic.

The Frantic Family – Technology was supposed to give us more leisure time, but just the opposite has happened. People are working harder than ever, which means they are spending less time at home being leisurely. Hahn and Verhaagen point out that because family members seem to be always "on the move," we have a new family reality: "more kinetic, less connected." (continued on next page)

The Floating Family – Because we feel less connected as families, we are more likely to look outside the family for support. We are looking elsewhere for those benefits the family used to give us: love, acceptance, support, and companionship. Consequently, it's not unusual for someone to comment that the people they work with are "like family." Studies show that only 19 percent of people in their twenties and thirties define a family in the traditional way: "a group of people to whom you are related by blood or marriage." They are much more likely to define a family as "people with whom you have close relationships or deep personal/emotional bonds."

A Perfect Family Bond

You can't change what has happened in the *past*, and there's little you can do to change your family *now*. So, in the rest of this chapter we want to concentrate on what you can do now to impact your future by building your own family foundation.

If you wanted to build a business, you wouldn't start from scratch and then, through trial and error, hope to come up with a plan that finally succeeded. By the time you finally figured out the best way to do business, you'd be out of business. Instead, you would study the current success stories to find a proven way of doing business, and then come up with a business model to serve as an example of how to do it right.

The same goes for building successful relationships, especially involving family. Don't use the "trial and error" method for connecting to people and building a network of relationships. By the time you figure it out, you'll be out of the relationship business. Instead, study current "success stories" to find a proven way of building a family foundation, and then follow it.

It just so happens that we have the perfect family model, one you can easily follow. Best of all, it's proven to work. That's because this family model, unlike the imperfect families we all come from, was given to us by God, who came up with the idea for family in the first place.

God is such a big fan of the family that he did more than just tell us how to live as families. God actually set the example by designing his eternal plan for us around the family model. Here's how it works.

God the Father

God has been called a lot of names we can greatly appreciate—loving, holy, just, forgiving, all-powerful, and all-knowing (plus a lot of Hebrew names we can't pronounce)—but the one name with which most of us can most identify is *Father*. Just look at these different ways God is our Father:

- He's the Father (Original Source) and Creator of all things (see 1 Corinthians 8:6).
- He's the Father of Israel, his chosen people (see Deuteronomy 32:6).
- He's the Father of Jesus the Son (see John 1:14, 18).
- He's the Father of his spiritual children (see Romans 8:15-16).

As our "heavenly Father," God has all the qualities an outstanding father should have:

- He loves us (see 1 John 4:11).
- He provides for us (see Matthew 6:32-33).
- He guides us (see Jeremiah 3:4).
- He corrects us (see Proverbs 3:12).
- He has compassion for us (see Psalm 103:13).

Perhaps your relationship with your earthly father hasn't been the best. Don't let that deter you. What you need to think about is the kind of father/parent you want to be. And then look to your heavenly Father.

Jesus the Son

Have you ever heard anyone say, "He looks just like his father" or, "She bears a striking resemblance to her parents"? When a child bears a likeness to his or her parents, it isn't just limited to looks. A child will have mannerisms and habits just like his or her mom or dad or both.

The person who bears the greatest resemblance to God is Jesus, his "only begotten Son" (John 3:16). In fact, the likeness is so exact that Jesus said, "When you see me, you've seen the Father" (see John 14:7). As a Son in both the spiritual sense (John 1:18) and the physical sense (Matthew 1:23), Jesus is an example to us of what the perfect son—and for that matter, the perfect child—should be like.

- He does the things that please his Father (see John 8:29).
- He brings glory to his Father (see John 17:1).
- He does his Father's will (see Matthew 26:39).

How does the example of Jesus the Son apply to you? No matter where you are in life, you never stop being a child, and you should never stop doing those things that bring honor to your parents (see Exodus 21:12).

The Children of God

Knowing that God is the Father and Jesus is the Son wouldn't have any meaning for us except for one thing—we can be adopted into God's family. When we are made right with God through faith in Jesus (see Galatians 3:24), God adopts us as his children, with all the rights and privileges therein.

> Now you are no longer a slave but God's own child. And since you are his child, everything he has belongs to you.
>
> GALATIANS 4:7

This is a very big concept. God isn't just some distant Father, and Jesus isn't some first-century philosopher. When you invite God into your life by believing in Jesus and what he did for you, you become a part of God's family as surely as you are part of an earthly family. You become a new person with a new life (see 2 Corinthians 5:17) and a new way of looking at your relationships.

A Practical Guide to Relating to Your Relations

Besides giving us the perfect family model, God has also given us some very practical advice for dealing with our families by being a good family member.

Husbands are to love their wives and wives are to respect their

(continued on next page)

husbands, just as Christ loves us (see Ephesians 5:32-33). As children, we should obey our parents because we belong to the Lord (see Ephesians 6:1). As parents, we need to raise our children "with the discipline and instruction approved by the Lord" (see Ephesians 6:4).

Your Personal Action Plan

You may not be able to change your family, but you can change the way you relate to your family. If you are a part of God's family and follow God's instructions for the family, your relations are going to improve dramatically—if you give yourself some time and follow this action plan.

1. Forgive and Forget. It doesn't matter if your family would make the list of "Top Ten Worst Families," or is scheduled to appear on the cover of Focus on the Family magazine. If you are holding any kind of resentment or bitterness in your heart toward anyone in your family, you need to forgive and forget.

Knowing that God has forgiven you should motivate you to forgive others, starting with your family. And if you're the one who needs to ask for forgiveness, don't hesitate to go to the parent you've offended or the sibling you've let down or the grandparent you've neglected and ask for forgiveness. You'll be amazed at how barriers will come down as you begin to connect with your family in new and energizing ways.

Understanding our adoption as sons and daughters of God allows us to forgive others, including family members, in ways that cut to our soul. We forgive deeply because we have been deeply, completely forgiven—and not only forgiven, but embraced and brought into an eternal family.

Todd Hahn and David Verhaagen

2. Move On and Move Out. Once you've forgiven and asked for forgiveness, move on. Even if you didn't get the response you were looking for, let it go. When God forgives you, he forgets about your sins and never stops loving you. We need to follow his example as we relate to others.

Moving on isn't the same as moving out, but in some cases it may have to be. There is a tendency today among young adults to come back home after being gone for a few years (they're called "boomerang kids"). There are some legitimate reasons for moving back home, but we can think of three that don't qualify: money, food, and laundry (please, tell us you're not still at home for those reasons).

If you are hanging around the house too long, more than likely you are doing so because, as Dr. James Dobson writes, "you don't know what to do next." If that's how you feel, think about this: The fact that you are still living at home may be the reason you are hesitant to move on in your life. Does your family seem to be experiencing extra tension? It may be there because you have overstayed your welcome.

Factoid

Fifty-three percent of adults 18–24 years old live at home, and 11 percent of adults 25–34 years old live at home. In the 25–34 age group, twice as many men as women live at home.

Perhaps you don't live at home, but you're about to hit the big 3-0 and you're still living with three roommates like you did when you were in college (and you're still wearing your old sweatpants like you did when you were in college). Maybe it's time you entered the real world of responsibility and relationships.

Unless you cut the umbilical cord and begin providing for yourself, you will remain in a state of arrested development.

Dr. James Dobson

Beginning to Build a Legacy

Just as surely as you inherited a heritage (the first part of your family foundation), you will leave a legacy (the other part of your family foundation). By definition, a legacy is something you hand down to your descendants, whether it's material possessions or your reputation. A legacy is a powerful thing that will testify to your existence in and your impact on the world.

Here's the great part: You don't have to wait until the day you die to leave your legacy. You can begin to build a legacy right now. It's your choice.

We're not going to advise you on the material part of your legacy. There is lots of great financial advice available to anyone who is willing to look, listen, and learn. Instead, we're going to give you a couple of final words on the reputation part of your family legacy and how it applies to your relationship network.

Why? When it's all said and done, the impact of your life will be measured more by the content of your character than by the extent of your wealth. The quality of your legacy will be determined by your network of family and friends, not your real estate portfolio. Yes, you should be diligent in your work and wise with your money. Just don't compromise your integrity, and never neglect your family.

Purely Single

If you're single, don't think you're off the hook when it comes to building a family legacy. Even if you don't have a family of your own right now, you may someday. Between now and then, don't do anything that you might regret later. Live a life of purity out of obedience to God and respect for others.

If marriage isn't in your future, you can still build into the lives and families of others. In our hometown there's a lady named Emma who never married. Even though she doesn't have any children of her own, she has probably had more influence on families and children than anyone else we know. Emma has been working with children through Child Evangelism Fellowship for more than seventy-five years. She started when she was in her twenties, and this past year Emma turned one hundred years old! Emma has touched the lives of tens of thousands of families by telling their children the Good News about God. What impact. What a legacy!

Faithfully Married

If you are married, soon to be married, or planning to be married, then you have the opportunity to build a family foundation that will directly impact your legacy. In a marriage, you have the potential to fill several family roles— as a spouse and in-law for sure, but also as a parent and perhaps someday a grandparent.

Above everything, remain as faithful to your family as you remain faithful to God. Don't let unfaithfulness spoil your legacy even a little. Ask God to help you be a person of integrity in all things.

We can tell you from experience that when you build a firm family foundation, the rest of your relationship network is stronger and more meaningful. In the next chapter we're going to look at the next phase of your relational construction project—friends.

CHAPTER 6

The Friendship Factor

L et's get one thing straight right from the start. This chapter is talking about serious friendships.

- Not the "I'm friends with the guy who lives across the street because he collects my newspapers when I'm out of town" kind of friendship;
- Not the "I'm going to the Rose Parade on New Year's Day and going to stay with a friend from college who lives in Pasadena" kind of friendship; and
- Not the "I'm going on one of those charity walks, so I have hit up all my friends at work to sponsor me" type of friendship.

Nope. You've got enough namby-pamby, fair-weather, here-today-gone-tomorrow kind of friends. You don't need any advice about collecting more of these. What we'll be talking about are the *real* friends in life. *Compadres.* Best buds. The kind of friends who:

- Say "yes" when you ask them for a favor, without making you say what it is before they answer;
- Double the excitement when you succeed, and shoulder half of your burden when you fail;

- Won't ask, "What'd ya do?" if you call in the middle of night from jail. They'll just ask, "Where do I come to get you?" (Of course, the ride home may allow for interesting dialogue between the two of you.)

If you have a few best friends, then consider yourself lucky. If you don't have any, then you need some.

Firm Foundations for Close Friendships

Close friendships are a little bit like the lottery. In the lottery, you can't win if you don't play, but you're not likely to win even when you do play. In relationships, you can't have a close friendship with people that you don't know (duh). But surprisingly, you're not likely to have a close friendship with the people that you do know.

What It Takes

Best friendships don't happen very often; it is a rare occurrence when all your quirks blend harmoniously with someone else's. Unfortunately, there is no single formula that produces "best friends," but there seem to be universal elements:

Common interests: Friendships often start because you have something in common with someone else. Maybe you work at the same office, attend the same church, or play on the same "weekend warriors" soccer team.

Similar characters: You can play soccer with just about anybody, but a friendship is likely to develop further only if you have a few character traits in common. This doesn't mean your respective personalities have to be identical. The extrovert can be a friend with the introvert, but it is unlikely that a person who reveres honesty will bond with a person who has a cavalier attitude about the truth.

Shared beliefs: Shallow friendships (or friendships at the initial stage of development) can survive in spite of differences of opinions, because they only

touch on innocuous subjects that nobody cares much about:
- Is Coke better than Pepsi?
- Is Letterman funnier than Leno?
- Would the Nordstrom shopping experience be the same without the piano guy?

Deeper friendships are forged with similar belief systems. You will have stronger relationships with those who agree with you about the importance of substantive issues (such as faith and family).

Sense of purpose: Even common interests, similar characters, and shared beliefs are not enough to forge a friendship that will endure through the many distractions of life. The most meaningful friendships also share a mutual sense of purpose. This doesn't mean that you both must volunteer to be missionaries in Africa or teach adult literacy programs in the Ozarks. It just means that you both must have a sense that your lives have meaning and significance beyond yourselves—that you both have a purpose in life—and that your respective purposes are taking you in similar directions.

You might be saying, "Hey! I'm just oozing character, beliefs, and purpose, but still I have diddly-squat in the 'best friends' department. What gives?" Well, we can think of three possible explanations for your plight:
- First of all, don't tell people that any part of you is oozing. We don't care that you are referring to a virtuous character trait. The "oozing" terminology conjures up a rather repulsive mental image that is a definite roadblock to friendship.
- Secondly, just having character, beliefs, and purpose isn't going to link you with anyone if you keep those aspects of your life incognito. Sure, you don't want to be blurting out your personal manifesto at an improper time or place (so stay off the company Intranet on your first day at work), but after a few years with the same gang they ought to know a little more about you than your opinions about Coke, Letterman, and Nordstrom.
- Thirdly, realize that you are not guaranteed a few "best friends" just because you can identify character, beliefs, and purpose in your life. All

meaningful friendships must have one additional ingredient: compatibility.

Getting Started

Selecting a best friend is not like choosing a ripe melon at the farmers' market or buying a puppy at the pet store. In those situations, the decision is all yours. When establishing friendships, you aren't in control. In fact, the more control you try to assert, the more you will drive people away from you. You'll be left sad and lonely (as we discussed in Chapter 1).

So, how should you start a friendship with the hope that it will become a meaningful relationship? Start by being the kind of friend you want to have.

If you want to have a best friend, you need to start being one.

Don't save your friendship behavior only for those candidates you want to enter your "Best Friends Sweepstakes." You need to be a friend to everyone in your network of connections. (The practice will do you good.) After all, because of that unpredictable "compatibility" factor, you never know who will end up winning the sweepstakes grand prize (that's you).

Three Faulty Friendship Factors

We have just discussed some of the factors that provide a firm foundation for a meaningful friendship. Now let's look at some other factors that bring people together but produce friendships with a few fatal flaws. Here is our list of three *wrong* reasons to be friends:

1. Don't pursue a relationship with people just because they make you look good. We are not prohibiting you from making friends with makeup artists, hair stylists, fashion designers, or plastic surgeons. We are suggesting that you avoid the trap of desiring a relationship with someone just because he or she is considered one of the "beautiful people." It's great when you are attracted to someone's personality and character qualities, but don't desire friendship with him (or her) just because that person has a certain kind of image. If this happens, you will always feel inferior (and they will always feel superior).

2. Don't waste your time in relationships where there is an ulterior motive. Be skeptical of that person who has snubbed you for years but now wants to be best friends with you. Sure, the attention is flattering, and you are pleased that this individual has finally matured enough to notice your fine qualities. But is the interest in your friendship sincere? Try to determine if this person has recently (a) obtained a license to sell insurance; (b) joined a cult; or (c) become an Amway distributor.

3. Common adversity can bring people together, but there is nothing left to hold them together after the adversity is gone. Tough times can produce a bond of friendship. (If you don't believe us, just watch any disaster movie and see how the romance develops between two protagonists once the volcano erupts, the asteroid hits, or the bomb explodes.) You may find yourself in a sudden friendship with others when you endure adversity together. Maybe it will happen when your company downsizes all of you out of a job. Or maybe it will be when you organize the homeowners' association against the developer of your townhouses. Whatever the scenario that brings you together, be prepared for the relationship to weaken when the crisis is over unless you have found some other connection to sustain your friendship.

To enjoy a friend, I need more in common with him than hating the same people.
Frank Clark

What's Love Got to Do With It?
Jesus placed a high value on having a small group of close friends. While he attracted large crowds of people (miracles tend to draw a crowd), he spent

quality time with only twelve men who comprised his gang of disciples. These men went through an amazing transformation during the three years that they spent with Jesus. At first, they were just regular guys. Get a mental picture of Jesus and the twelve disciples as they walked together from town to town:

- James and John are arguing about who can cast a fishing net the farthest.
- Matthew is asking if anyone has a toothpick. He has just eaten a locust dipped in honey (a delicacy that John the Baptist recommended), and he needs to dislodge the locust leg that got caught between his teeth.
- Peter is scratching his left armpit with his right hand, and as he moves his arm, he becomes the first guy to invent those armpit noises that have been entertaining men ever since.

Do you get the idea? These were just plain old guys. They weren't overly "religious," they weren't sophisticated, and they certainly weren't in touch with their feminine side. Ordinarily, regular guys don't "bond" with each other like these men did.

But these guys had something special in common (and it wasn't impeccable hygiene). They had Jesus in their group. For the first time in history, mankind had a human representation of God's love. After being exposed to the love of Jesus for three years, this ragtag band of men had developed a love for each other that helped them change the direction of history.

Jesus was a role model for his disciples. He displayed great love toward them, and he told them to love each other in the same way:

So now, I am giving you a new commandment: Love each other. Just as I have loved you, you should love each other.

JOHN 13:34

Jesus wasn't talking about some kind of romantic love (we'll get to that in Chapter 7). This is a "best friend" kind of love. If you're interested in making best friend relationships and keeping them, you'll want to examine some of the characteristics of this kind of love.

Five Qualities of a True Friend:
An Inside Perspective

Let's look at some of the qualities of love (the true friendship kind) listed in 1 Corinthians 13. This is the famous "love chapter" written by the apostle Paul. Look at these qualities. See if they pinpoint the exact character traits that you would want in a friend. Do they describe the kind of person you would like to be—on the inside—so that you could be a best friend to someone?

• **A friend is trusting.** Best friends can relax in their friendship because they trust each other. You don't have to count your change when your friend brings it back from the cashier. But more important than that, you have confidence that your friend will keep your personal matters private. We're talking about more important stuff than the fact that you don't want the secret about your nose job blabbed all over town. We're talking about the hopes, dreams, and struggles you've shared with your friend.

If either of you doesn't trust the other, then your friendship won't grow very deep because you will stay on "safe" subjects and not discuss the personal issues that mean the most to you.

• **A friend is not envious.** It's easy to be sympathetic when something bad happens. Even casual friends will be there to give you a little comfort and encouragement when you lose your job, get in an accident, or experience the death of a family member. But these same people won't be genuinely friendly when you get a promotion or get an envelope from Ed McMahon that actually contains the winning sweepstakes number.

This contradiction is easy to explain: Most people find it easier to be sympathetic over someone's sorrow than happy about another person's good fortune. That's when envy raises its ugly head. They want the good stuff for themselves.

Not so with a true friend. Your best friends will be excited when good things happen in your life. They are not in competition with you—they consider themselves to be on "your" team.

• **A friend keeps no record of being wronged.** Friends at a shallow stage in their friendship spend a lot of time keeping score.

"I've paid for the last two lunches."

"I've called three times in a row."

"She's picked the movie every time but twice."

"This is the twenty-seventh time I've been over to his house to watch football games on Sunday afternoon, and he has never had those potato chips with the ridges, and he knows I like those ridges."

It's never the important stuff you keep score of, just stupid stuff. (If it were important, then you wouldn't keep hanging around together.) But best friendships don't have scoreboards (or even pocket score pads). Those little things don't matter because the friendship itself is so important that you don't want the little things to be in the way. You just forget about them (the little things, not the friends).

For example, in our friendship, Bruce totally ignores the fact that Stan and his wife Karin never serve the chips with ridges to Bruce and his wife Cheryl.

•**A friend believes the best and expects the best.** Most people don't have a very high regard for those they don't know very well. Best friendships are forged when you know and respect each other's character (because you wouldn't be best friends with someone who you didn't respect and couldn't trust). You want an example? Let's say someone was spreading a rumor that you had done something despicable.

An acquaintance would say: "This is interesting. Tell me more."

Your best friend would reply: "I don't believe it. It doesn't sound like him. And I won't believe it unless he tells me himself."

When your best friend has that kind of expectation about you, it makes you want to live up to it.

•**A friend is loyal, no matter what.** Dogs are loyal because you feed them, but you can't depend on them to feed *you*. Fair-weather friends are pretty much the same way. They hang around when things are going well, but they somehow vanish when the going gets tough for you. A true friend, a real friend, will stick by you even though it is of great sacrifice.

— *Your best friends won't participate in gossip about you,* even if it means being ostracized from a group because they offended others by defending you.

— *Your best friends won't abandon you* when you are sick or depressed (and basically no fun to be with for a while).

— And most important of all, *your best friends will stick by you when you really screw up* and have actually done that despicable thing. (Hey, all along they knew you weren't perfect, and they liked you anyway.)

A Mistaken Notion of Friendship

"I'm a very dependable friend.
You can always count on my being around when I need you."

We're sure that these qualities from 1 Corinthians 13 are exactly what you would like to find in a friend. But don't think that you can find someone like that and immediately forge a best friendship. Remember that you must first be that kind of person on the inside yourself, because the other person will want to see those qualities in you.

Five Supportive Actions Between Friends:
An Outside Perspective

As you develop the inner qualities of 1 Corinthians 13, a funny thing will happen. (Not "ha-ha" funny, "interesting" funny.) Your conduct and actions will begin to change. You'll begin to find that you are actually giving more of yourself to your friends and to others around you. You'll begin to notice that you are less and less concerned about yourself, and more and more concerned about your friends.

Below is a short list of some characteristics of true friendship that we think you'll start to notice in your life. (Before you read it you should know that we didn't make this list up. We found these characteristics in the Bible. More than seventy times in the New Testament there are descriptions of the actions that we should display "to one another" if we say that we have the love of God in us.)

• **Friends accept each other.** When you are accepting, you refuse to let peculiarities and idiosyncrasies irritate you. You learn to appreciate differences in others without letting them divide you.

> May God, who gives this patience and encouragement, help you live in complete harmony with each other.... So accept each other just as Christ has accepted you.
>
> ROMANS 15:5-7

• **Friends encourage each other.** Friends have a kind of power over each other. You can use that power to build each other up or to tear each other down.

> Let everything you say be good and helpful, so that your words will be an encouragement to those who hear them.
>
> EPHESIANS 4:29

• **Friends forgive each other.** Our natural reaction is to hold a grudge when someone offends us. (Come on, admit it. We like that feeling of righteous indignation.) But that is not how friends should treat one another. They should be quick to forgive.

> Be kind to each other, tenderhearted, forgiving one another, just as God through Christ has forgiven you.
>
> EPHESIANS 4:32

• **Friends serve each other.** Immature friendships are based on what the *other* person can do for you. In meaningful relationships, friends look for opportunities to serve each other. True friends don't consider themselves "too important" to do things for each other.

> For you have been called to live in freedom—not freedom to satisfy your sinful nature, but freedom to serve one another in love.
>
> GALATIANS 5:13

• **Friends support each other.** Oh, if we wanted to sound biblical about this, we would be talking about "bearing one another's burdens" (but we think that sounds like carrying your friend's laundry tub to the Fluff 'N' Fold). Instead, think of it as being available to each other when tough times hit. Sometimes that means helping out; other times that means just being available to listen and understand each other.

> So don't get tired of doing what is good. Don't get discouraged and give up.... Whenever we have the opportunity, we should do good to everyone, especially to our Christian brothers and sisters.
>
> GALATIANS 6:9-10

Five Ways to Kill a Friendship

Sometimes it is easier to explain something by describing the opposite. We think that it might be interesting (but you'll be the ultimate judge of that) to look at a few characteristics that can *kill* a friendship. You can take this list either way. If you want to bring an existing friendship to a quick termination, here's what you should do. Or, if you're looking to keep a friendship going, then here's what *not* to do:

1. Be intrusive. If there is something your friend doesn't want you to know, be a pest about it. Don't stop with just being interested and asking a few benign questions. Make it a real interrogation.

2. Be intolerant. Don't accept any differences. Insist that your friend conform to your standards. (Oh, and don't forget to be very judgmental about it. That'll help, too.)

3. Be independent. Make sure your friends know that you don't really need them. Do a lot of activities without even telling them. Make sure that they feel they are a dispensable part of your life. Do nothing that displays thoughtfulness toward them. They need to realize that you are slightly attached to them but that they have no purpose in your life—like a wart.

4. Be insensitive. Look for ways to say things that will be hurtful. This can best be accomplished by finding a physical flaw that your friend is self-conscious about. Make a lot of jokes about it. Doing this in public, with a lot of pointing and laughing, is particularly effective.

5. Be introspective. Let's be truthful. Life is all about *you*. Other people don't really matter, except that they should be focused on you. Bring every conversation around to your situation. Don't waste time talking about any-one else's circumstances. Everyone's life will be much more interesting if you are the center of attention.

You can make more friends in two months
by becoming interested in other people
than you can in two years
by trying to get other people interested in you.
Dale Carnegie

The Serious Side of Friendship

We're sure that you're getting the notion that friendships take a lot of work. But wait. We haven't even gotten to the most difficult part yet. There are two additional aspects essential to every meaningful relationship. These are tough to do, but your friendships will always stay on the shallow side unless you and your friends are willing to make these commitments to each other.

Accountability
When you were much younger, you had a parent with a checklist to make sure that you handled all of the essential hygienic activities of the morning: toilet, teeth, face, hands, and nose (but probably not in that order). Now that you're older, you don't need someone who monitors your bathroom activities (hopefully), but you do need someone in your life who cares enough about you to hold you accountable for what you both know you should be

doing (and shouldn't be doing).

Accountability is a rare trait among friends. Often we don't want to hold our friends accountable because we don't want them to hold us to a similar standard. But accountability is essential, and it works only if everyone commits to it.

Confrontation

If you have trouble telling a friend when there's a piece of spinach wedged between his front teeth, how are you going to confront him when he's really screwed up and is refusing to see it or admit it? Difficult or not, you've got to do it.

Confrontation is the flip side of accountability. Accountability between friends is a way to encourage right living; confrontation occurs when one of them has stepped over the line. Accountability may be tough, but confrontation is even harder. And like accountability, confrontation only works when everyone is committed to it.

The success of a confrontation depends on the attitude of the people involved. The person who initiates the confrontation should have an attitude that goes something like this: "This is difficult for me to say; I wish I didn't have to say it, but you need to hear it." The person who is on the receiving end of the dialogue needs to be willing to graciously accept criticism.

**Confrontation is always dangerous and difficult,
but it is the ultimate test—and proof—of true friendship.**

Still Lonely Among Friends?

Once you have established meaningful relationships with some friends, all of your social problems won't be solved. In fact, you'll have a new set of challenges, and "balance" may be one of them. Meaningful friendships require a lot of time, and you'll have to juggle your activities, commitments, and friends (without dropping any of them). Here are three important principles to keep in mind:

• *If you have too many "best" friends, you run the risk of spreading yourself too thin.* You probably don't have to worry about having too many "best" friends. We aren't suggesting that you're too repulsive to be well-liked. We just know that your schedule probably doesn't allow it. You'll go crazy if you attempt to develop meaningful relationships with too many people all at the same time. You'll be putting yourself under tremendous pressure, and none of your friends will have the "best" part of you.

• *Too few friends can make you too dependent.* On the other hand, you do need to develop several meaningful relationships. Don't put all of your time and energy into a single person. Otherwise you run the risk of smothering your friend and restricting your own personal growth.

• *A friendship with the opposite sex can be the opposite of sex.* Don't make the mistake of thinking that you can only establish a "best friend" relationship with a person of your own gender. This has to be the case for people in a convent or a monastery, but that's not *you* because *you* hang out at the condo and the mall. So, you're likely to meet people of the opposite sex.

As we discussed in Chapter 2, sitcom life portrays every guy-gal relationship as being all about sex. Well, real life doesn't have to be that way. A man and a woman can have a deep friendship without all of those sexual overtones. Of course, you may be looking for a relationship with a member of the opposite sex that moves from the platonic to the romantic. Maybe you're looking for a relationship that grows from engaging to engagement. If so, read this chapter again, because establishing a good friendship is the best foundation for a good marriage. Then, read the next chapter where we talk about finding the love of your life.

CHAPTER 7

Love, Romance, and Connections of the Spousal Kind

I f you just skipped Chapters 1 through 6 to get to this one, welcome. In our humble (but correct) opinion, you've missed a lot of important insights if you skipped the first few chapters. But maybe you did the right thing by skipping ahead because you wouldn't have paid much attention to that other stuff, anyway. Hey, you've got one thing on your mind, and you want us to get right to it. So we will. (Maybe then your mind will be free to go back to the first six chapters of the book!)

Love, romance, and passion predominate out culture, and for good reason. Almost everyone is interested in them. However, most people are so anxious to find a meaningful relationship with a member of the opposite sex that they embark on that quest without any planning. That goes against the whole thesis of this book (which you would know by now if you had read Chapters 1 though 6). Your relationships should be intentionally designed.

This is absolutely essential when you are choosing a spouse, but you shouldn't start the game plan only when you've got marriage on your mind. You need to start making deliberate choices at the early dating stage. Why?

Your spouse will probably be someone whom you have been dating. So, you should be as intentional about your dates as you would be in choosing a spouse—any date could be your future mate. (Of course, this won't be true if you are a mail-order bride or if you get married to a stranger as a stunt on a TV game show—in which case you'd be better off coming in second and taking home the lovely consolation gifts.)

In this chapter, we are going to lead you by the hand through the topics of dating and premarital relationships (we have noticed that this topic makes your palms sweaty). We'll be giving you some straight talk about you—in particular, what changes you may have to make to prepare yourself for these relationships. And we'll be talking about the kind of person you might want to be looking for.

Unfortunately, we don't know whether you are a male or female reader, so we don't know if we should be referring to your *boyfriend* or your *girlfriend*. So, we'll just give a generic name to the *other person* in your relationship. Let's call that person **"Chris."** If you are a guy, think of her as Christine; if you're a gal, think of him as Christopher.

As you read the pages that follow, think about yourself and your relationship with "Chris." We think you might get pretty excited about the prospects. (And if there is a God in heaven—which there is—maybe Chris will be reading a copy of this book. Then the two of you will be perfectly prepared for each other.)

This "Guy-Girl" Thing Was All God's Idea

The Hollywood culture has certainly distorted the concept of love and passion, but the original concept was divinely designed. God's original plan for the human race included a permanent relationship between a man and woman who would live together for the rest of their lives as husband and wife. But don't take our word for it. Here is how Moses explained the genesis of marriage (pun intended):

- After God had created the earth and all the animals, he created Adam. Adam was given the responsibility for naming the animals. In that process, a funny thing happened. Adam started noticing that there were a Mr. and a Mrs. of each type of animal, but there was no Mrs. Adam to be found in the Garden of Eden. This made Adam kind of mopey, so God said: "It is not good for man to be alone" (Genesis 2:18).

- Interestingly, God didn't solve the problem of Adam's loneliness by giving him a TV set (or at least not one with ESPN). This is a point that should be emphasized to many husbands and boyfriends. God said, "I will make a companion who will help him" (Genesis 2:18). Notice that God's solution was a *companion*—not a maid, or a servant or slave (another point that should not go unnoticed by many husbands and boyfriends).
- God really knows how to solve a problem. He didn't make just any kind of best buddy as a companion for Adam. We have a much more creative and romantic God than that. He created a *woman* (see Genesis 2:22) who just happened to be anatomically designed to be fully (and pleasurably) compatible with Adam.
- God obviously knew what would appeal to Adam, because the first glimpse of Eve caused Adam to exclaim: "At last!" (Genesis 2:23). According to our research, this was the first—and to this day the only— *articulate* expression that any member of the male species has uttered in the presence of a woman to whom he was attracted.
- There was more than physical attraction involved here. God's plan for the man and the woman entailed a lifetime union that would bind them together emotionally, physically, and spiritually.

This explains why a man leaves his father and mother and is joined to his wife, and the two are united into one.

GENESIS 2:24

When Jesus quoted this verse, he gave this additional explanation:

Since they are no longer two but one, let no one separate them, for God has joined them together.

MATTHEW 19:5-6

The fact that God designed marriage for a man and a woman doesn't mean that *any* man should marry *any* woman, and vice versa. The pairing of Adam with Eve was rather obvious (because there were no alternatives for them).

God wants you to be selective. Maybe Chris is the person you should marry, maybe not. In the following pages we'll give you some help for making that decision.

Marriages are made in heaven, but so are thunderstorms, tornadoes, and hurricanes.

Marriage Is Not For Everyone

One of God's purposes for marriage was to facilitate the population of the earth. Or to say it in biblical terms: Be fruitful and multiply (see Genesis 1:28). Well, Adam and Eve and their progeny did a pretty good job of that, and the world is now amply covered with people.

Did God design marriage for everyone? The answer is a resounding "No." Singleness is an option that shouldn't be viewed as second-class status. Jesus didn't marry, and he didn't command his disciples to do it. In fact, the apostle Paul was unmarried, and he indicated that singleness might be a preferred option for some people (see 1 Corinthians 7:8). Paul might have been single by his own choice. We have a sneaking suspicion, however, that most women were turned off because he was frequently arrested and occasionally stoned by angry mobs. Those are two factors that aren't conducive to romance.

Dating: Kiss It Goodbye or Hug It Hello?

You might be thinking that dating is the first stage of romance. Well, you'd be wrong. It's not the first stage at all; it is more like the fourth stage. The first three are:

- **Stage 1: "I Like What I See."** If you and Chris are like most couples, one of you noticed the other first. You may have even known each other before, but there was an initial moment when one of you looked at the other with at least a twinge of romantic interest (those twinges are great moments).
- **Stage 2: "Do You See Me?"** Those romantic twinges must cause some type of bio-chemical or physiological dysfunction. As soon as they happen, you start doing some goofy things so the person you're interested in notices you. You might not do these things on purpose; they might be subconscious. How else can women explain tripping on a chair (which never happens otherwise) or laughing convulsively at a joke that isn't funny? Guys aren't any more suave as they walk around flexing their pecs and clenching their cheeks (and we aren't talking about their facial muscles). You end up looking rather spastic, but at least you draw attention to yourself.
- **Stage 3: "Well, Hellooooo."** The intensity of the romance really cranks up at Stage 3 as initial verbal contact is established. The intent is always witty, but the result is usually witless. But that's OK. This dialogue is a necessary cultural component because it provides stand-up comedians with lots of material.

We think you'll recognize (and identify with) these initial stages of romance. You first saw them in junior high school, and they have been repeated by you and your contemporaries ever since. Once you get past Stage 3, your budding romance with Chris is ready to move to the dating stage. But hold on. Should you be dating at all?

The "To Date or Not to Date" Debate

Some people have been rejecting the concept of dating. Joshua Harris championed this viewpoint in his book, *I Kissed Dating Goodbye*. He identified several "negative tendencies" of dating:

1. Dating leads to intimacy but not necessarily to commitment.
2. Dating tends to skip the "friendship" stage of a relationship.
3. Dating often mistakes a physical relationship for love.
4. Dating often isolates a couple from other vital relationships.

5. Dating, in many cases, distracts young adults from their primary responsibility of preparing for the future.
6. Dating can cause discontent with God's gift of singleness.
7. Dating creates an artificial environment for evaluating another person's character.

We agree that these problems can exist when dating is not done properly. We just don't think dating should be abandoned because problems are caused when it's done improperly. (The expression about "throwing the baby out with the bath water" comes to mind.) Instead, we think that the *proper approaches* to dating should be emphasized.

If you and Chris are dating *in the appropriate context,* you can avoid the negatives that Joshua Harris identifies while enjoying some very significant benefits:

- Dating will give you the opportunity to learn more about yourself.
- Dating will give you the opportunity to learn about interpersonal relationships with the opposite sex.
- Dating can give you an opportunity to learn sexual self-control.
- Dating will allow you to identify the character qualities that you desire in a future spouse.
- Dating can be a lot more fun than sitting alone in your apartment on Friday night, watching "Gilligan's Island" on Nick at Nite.

So What Is the Appropriate Context for Dating?

Notice that we are proponents of dating within an appropriate context. Perhaps you are wondering what those parameters might be. Since you asked, we'll tell you.

- *Guard Your Mind:* You'll enjoy dating Chris much more if you have decided ahead of time the values that are important to you. We are sure that you're interested in honesty, integrity, kindness, and respect (to name a few). These are values that you want to display in your life, and you will want them to be exhibited in Chris' life as well. You can avoid many of the negative aspects of dating if you have the right mind-set going into each date. Your faith, values, and beliefs should set the parameters for each date.

- *Guard Your Heart:* Unless you're careful, the romance of dating can catch you by surprise. You need to stay in control of your own feelings. Be diligent. Don't let your emotions commandeer your rational thinking. And don't be unreasonably impacted by Chris' emotions. While you want to be sensitive to what Chris is feeling, you can't let Chris' sentiments or moods override your judgment.
- *Guard Your Body:* The appropriate context for dating requires a predetermined boundary for your behavior. Set your standards for how you will act before you enter into a dating relationship. The time to determine your boundaries is when you can reflect quietly and calmly about them. Don't wait until you are passionately entangled to set the standards for your behavior.

It's hard to guard your heart if someone already has hold of your body.

A Few Practical Guidelines

Don't think that the concept of guarding your mind, heart, and body is purely theoretical. There are some practical guidelines that can be of real help to you in establishing an appropriate context for a dating relationship with Chris.

Don't think of these guidelines as rules. A list of "don'ts" is the wrong approach to dating (because it encourages you to look for loopholes and exceptions). Instead of focusing on prohibited behavior, think about the positive aspects of your relationship.

- *Treat each other with respect.* Remember that Chris might be someone else's future spouse. How would that future spouse want you to be treating Chris on your date? (That's an easier question to answer if you realize that someone else might be dating your future spouse right now. How do you want that person to treat the individual you will eventually marry?)
- *Treat yourself with respect.* Don't let anyone take you for granted. You deserve to be respected and admired. Don't feel that you have to

grovel, or beg, or whine for attention. If you aren't appreciated, then respect yourself enough to bring this particular dating relationship to a quick end.

- *Realize that your greatest emotional needs will not be satisfied in a dating relationship.* You are a complex individual. While Chris may hold a prominent role in your life, Chris cannot fill the voids in your life. You need to achieve balance on your own. This involves finding your own meaning and purpose in life (more about this in Chapter 11), independent of Chris. Once your own life is in order, you will be better able to enjoy a relationship that isn't inappropriately dependent upon Chris' approval or acceptance of you.

Love may be blind, but it shouldn't be deaf and dumb.

The Spousal Search: Who Are the Likely Candidates?

If you wind up marrying the first person you date, you are the exception to the rule. It is far more likely that for you, dating will be a process of elimination—enjoying a person's company and learning from the dating relationship, while realizing that God didn't intend for you to become lifetime partners. In our view, this is a very valid purpose of dating. As you mature in the dating process, you will get progressively more selective because you know more about the type of person you are looking for in a spouse.

Custom Design Your Spouse

You don't need to compile a computerized database, but you should be doing something more than just making mental notes about what you like and dislike about your previous dates. Be thoughtful about the type of person you would consider as spousal material. In fact, make a profile for this person.

When we say, "write a profile," we aren't talking about drawing a caricature of facial features and body type. You can leave hair color, weight, and height off the list, too. This spousal profile will include the type of character and qualities that you want your future spouse to possess.

You can't custom design the profile for your future spouse unless you have first identified the character traits and values that are important to you. Your analysis of your personal beliefs should touch on issues such as:

- Your personal faith in God
- Your life's purpose (or what you find meaningful in life)
- The importance you place on relationships with others (and how those relationships are maintained)
- The role of your family in your life
- How you handle your finances (and your whole attitude toward possessions and wealth)
- Your interest in and commitment to social issues
- Whether you are planning to have children (and what your approach will be in raising them)

Once you have thought through these issues, you'll have a much easier time knowing whether Chris is a serious prospect for a future spouse. While you may enjoy Chris' company and companionship, you're likely to cross Chris off the spousal prospect list if you have major differences of opinion about the most important issues in your life.

Guidelines for Spousal Selection

Between us, we don't have a lot of experience in selecting spouses: We've done it a total of two times (once by Bruce and once by Stan). But we must have been pretty good at it, because each of our respective marriages has endured the test of time. (If you knew our wives, you would realize that we are experts at spousal selection, although you would question *their* ability in this regard.)

Here are a few of our guidelines for selecting a spouse:

1. *Marry the person you can't live without.* There are lots of people you could live with. But only one that you can't live without. Marry that one.

2. *Don't marry someone you're planning to change.* During dating and engagement, everyone is on his or her best behavior, and the romance

tends to moderate some offensive characteristics. After marriage, the problems become more apparent as the romance fades, and people aren't as careful to maintain their good behavior.

3. *Don't pick a spouse too soon.* Remember that you're in a process of developing and maturing in your own beliefs and attitudes. Don't commit to someone too soon, as your spousal criteria might drastically shift after you gain more life experience.

4. *Don't marry too fast.* Get to know as much as possible about the person you are considering spending the rest of your life with. A quick romance and engagement often precludes seeing your prospective spouse in a variety of circumstances and situations. Also, developing the kind of deep relationship that is foundational to a marriage commitment requires both *quality* time and *quantity* time.

5. *Marry only someone who shares your commitment to a lifelong marriage.* Your marriage is very vulnerable if either one of you thinks that the marriage can end if "things don't work out." Have no contingency plans. This attitude will force you to straighten out the problems in your marriage because neither of you will have any other place (or person) to go to.

6. *Hold firm to your spiritual beliefs and make sure they are shared with your potential spouse.* In biblical terms it is expressed this way: "Don't be unequally yoked" (2 Corinthians 6:14). Marriages take two people, pulling side by side. That can't happen if each of you doesn't place the same priority on your relationship with God.

7. *Most importantly, don't settle.* Don't ever think, "No one will want me so I better be willing to compromise on the character qualities that I'm looking for." Once God has guided you in compiling a profile of your future spouse, don't settle for less than God's best just because you are getting impatient.

Choose wisely.
Yoda

Love: How Do You Know If It's the Real Thing?

Wouldn't it be great if there were some type of test you could take to determine if you were really in love and ready for marriage? Some kind of X-ray or cardiac sonogram would do nicely. Anything objective that could tell you—for certain—whether this particular person was "the one."

Well, there isn't any such objective "litmus" test, mechanical or otherwise, so give it up. (And don't even think about using one of those fortune-telling eight balls. When you flip them upside down, the little sign on the bottom always gets stuck sideways, and you can never get a good reading.) Even so, there are some *subjective* tests that can help you determine if you're dealing with true love and are ready for marriage, or whether that queasy feeling is just excess stomach acid.

In his book *How to Know If You're Really In Love* Charlie Shedd lists ten tests that can help you determine if you are dealing with "marriageable" love. These test questions might be helpful to you. (Actually, the questions won't help you, but the answers—*your* answers—will.) As with all tests, no cheating. Honesty counts. After all, this is your life that you're dealing with here.

1. **The Transparency Test:** Do the two of you really want to be transparent with each other? Are you interested in communicating at a deep level to reveal information about yourself and find out more about Chris?

2. **The Liberty Test:** Do you give each other enough room to move around, to grow individually, and to develop a healthy independence? Do you give each other space in your togetherness?

3. **The Unselfishness Test:** Are you in this relationship because Chris offsets your own shortcomings? If so, then perhaps your motives are selfish. Marriageable love is interested in the other person just because the other person is who he or she is. Are you in love with who Chris is, or because of what Chris does for you?

4. **The Mercy Test:** Do you forgive each other? Is your relationship mature enough to recognize that neither of you is perfect and that both of you have done things in the past, and will do things in the future, that will require forgiveness? When these situations occur, can they be discussed openly? Is there a spirit of compassion, or does one of you become judgmental?

5. **The Apology Test:** This is the flip side of the Mercy Test. When one of you extends forgiveness, is the other willing to offer a sincere apology? Is each of you willing to admit when you are wrong? And is the admission accompanied by regret and by an honest attempt to avoid repeating the same mistake in the future?

6. **The Sexuality Test:** Is the passion expressed between you a matter of self-gratification, or is it a tender display of your respect for each other? Does the sexual aspect of your relationship overshadow equally essential components of true love? While physical attraction is an important part of your relationship, you should not ignore the mental, emotional, and spiritual aspects of your friendship.

> Don't think of sex as just two bodies touching. Think of it as two lives coming together. (Maybe that is why so many couples receive blenders as wedding gifts.)

7. **The Money Test:** Do you each have a similar philosophy toward finances, or are your differences going to drive you apart?

8. **The Distance Test:** Do you have compatible views of the future? As you look down the road of life, do you see similar situations and circumstances for you as a couple? Do you share the same future perspective on things such as your careers, your family, and your need for each other's companionship?

9. **The Fun Test:** Yes, you both like to laugh and have fun, but do you enjoy the same things in life? Can you do things together that bring a sense of well-being to both of you? Do you find physical, mental, and spiritual refreshment in things that you can do together?

10. **The Holiness Test:** Are the two of you spiritually compatible? If not, then you have to wonder whether you have a marriageable love. Your faith in God should be the part of your relationship where you share the most in common, because it will be the source of your greatest strength as a couple.

> There are three things that amaze me—no, four things I do not understand:
> How an eagle glides through the sky,
> How a snake slithers on a rock,
> How a ship navigates the ocean,
> How a man loves a woman.
>
> PROVERBS 30:18-19

Getting Physical: Keeping Sex Where It Belongs

The physical aspect of your dating relationships and engagement is very important, and it deserves to be discussed. But we are two guys, right? (Take our word for it.) So, as you might expect, we get a little flustered talking frankly about, well, you know ... sex. There, we said it (and it was just as uncomfortable as we thought it would be).

In our first draft of this chapter, we tried to condense (meaning, we tried to avoid) this discussion with the following single statement:

**Sex is a great gift from God.
But he designed it for enjoyment by a husband and wife
in their marriage. That's where it belongs.**

But our pesky editor, Heidi, said: "Oh, no, you don't. You can't get away that easy. A frank discussion about sex may offend *your* sensibilities, but it needs to be addressed. So, don't blush and run!"

You know, Heidi was right. (We hate when that happens.) So, at the risk of embarrassing ourselves, we'll raise some issues that you ought to be thinking about.

1. Sex was designed by God. God is certainly no sexually repressed prude. He is the One who thought up the idea of sex in the first place. How do we know? Well, he designed and created the male and female bodies. And his design made those two bodies—how shall we say it—anatomically compatible. And those two bodies fit together in a fashion that is incredibly pleasurable.

The whole idea of sex was not just for procreation and population of the earth. (He could have arranged for pregnancy to occur by the male and female simultaneously snapping their fingers, but that wouldn't have been nearly as much fun.) God knew what he was doing when he made sexual intercourse so pleasurable, and all we have to say is: "Thank you, God."

2. Sex ought to be used the way it was designed, and that means within marriage. Go back and read the first few pages of this chapter where we discussed that guy-girl relationships were God's idea. (Go on; we'll wait.) Notice the reference to Genesis 2:24 to the two being "united into one." The old King James Version terminology is "become one flesh." This is a bonding of all aspects of the two persons—emotional, spiritual, mental—but also the physical. And there is nothing that makes you "one flesh" more than the intimacy of sexual intercourse. But also notice that the reference is in the context of a husband and a wife. Whenever the Bible talks about the pleasure and blessing of sexual intercourse, it is within the context of marriage. Whenever the Bible talks about the dangers and disasters of sexual intercourse, it is always within the context of sex outside of marriage.

OK, so far we haven't told you anything that you haven't heard before. And maybe you already subscribe to the "No Sex Until Marriage" principle. We hope so. But let's get honest for a moment. Are you looking for a loophole? Are you looking for a technical definition of "sex" that will allow you to mess around without "crossing the line"? Are you thinking that oral sex is OK and doesn't disqualify you as a "virgin" because your respective genitals have not touched simultaneously? (This is probably more brutal honesty than Heidi expected.) Here's what we have to say about that:

- *Don't look for loopholes and technicalities to God's principles.* The whole point is that God intends sexual intimacy to be reserved for marriage. There are many variations and degrees of physical touching that can be just as intimate as intercourse.
- *God's principle of loving each other demands respect for each other.* Often, physical intimacy (even of the nonintercourse type) is driven by a desire

for self-gratification. It makes you feel good, and you don't even care much what is happening with the other person. That is contrary to God's principle of putting the other person's feelings ahead of your own.

- *Until you are married, there is a chance that you may break up.* As with intercourse, other activities of the heavy-breathing variety should be reserved for marriage because they are so intimate. That kind of intimacy should be shared only between a husband and a wife. And while you might expect that a relationship is "the real thing," you won't know for sure until you say, "I do." Don't you want a spouse who hasn't had that kind of intimacy with anyone else but you? Don't you think your future spouse would feel the same way about you?

- *Self-control before marriage helps you exhibit self-control after marriage.* Much of life entails self-control. The apostle Paul taught that it is pleasing to God when we learn to control our bodies and live in holiness and honor instead of lustful passion (see 1 Thessalonians 4:4-5). Self-control doesn't just happen. It needs to be developed. If you can't learn to control your "sexual urges" before you are married, what makes you think that you can control them after the wedding?

  From the honeymoon on, you and your spouse will enjoy the physical intimacy of your marriage, but that doesn't mean that all sexual temptation will disappear from your life. You may be faced with a whole new set of physical temptations—including the possibility of entertaining sexual thoughts and engaging in actions with someone other than your spouse. Don't expect that sexual self-control will get easier after marriage; in many respects, it gets more difficult. Therefore, you may want to start working on the discipline of self-control now.

Each of us dated his wife for about four years before we were married, and as couples we were committed to remaining "pure" before marriage (to get back to that old King James Version terminology). So, we know exactly what you are thinking at this point: "If we can't have sex, then what can we do?" Good question, and we know that "a rousing game of chess" is not the answer you are looking for.

As your relationship develops, particularly during your engagement, there will likely be a progression in your intimacy. That is good and natural, but you may want to work at keeping the progression gradual. The Bible doesn't condemn passion, but it does criticize *lustful* passion (see 1 Thessalonians 4:5 again). We think that is the key. If your passion is out of control, if it is self-centered, or if it becomes a disproportionate emphasis in your relationship, then you are going too far.

Most couples (or at least the guys) strategize about "how far" they can go in their sexual explorations without going too far. They want to get as close to the line as possible without crossing over it. Maybe it would be helpful to focus on what the two of you can do to stay as close to God as possible. After all, since he is the inventor and designer of your sex mechanisms, maybe you ought to follow his plan for maximum enjoyment of the equipment.

If you want to know more about S-E-X, we're glad to refer you to two excellent books that deal with romance and dating:
- *Finding the Love of Your Life* by Dr. Neil Clark Warren
- *Boundaries in Dating* by Dr. Henry Cloud and Dr. John Townsend

---

Before You Say "I Do"

There are lots of jokes about the prospective bride or groom getting "cold feet." We aren't too worried about circulatory flow to your lower extremities. We are more concerned that there be adequate blood flow to your brain. Amidst the romantic thoughts, make sure you leave some time for rational thinking.

We strongly recommend that you and Chris receive some premarital counseling before the wedding. And don't wait until the week before the ceremony. Start as soon as you get engaged. Your pastor or priest will probably be glad to spend several sessions with you.

The purpose of premarital counseling is to help you consider the significance of marriage in a rational context, removed from the heat of your passion and the euphoria of the romance. It's hard to think clearly when you're lip-locked in a passionate embrace or romanticizing a "happily ever after" life. The counselor can help you ask the questions that you might otherwise want to avoid—questions that you think are too mundane—or questions that you don't want to answer because you know they might lead to significant differences of opinion.

Even without a counselor, you owe it to yourself (and to Chris) to ask some probing questions. This list isn't exhaustive, but it is enough to get you started. We suggest that you and Chris answer these questions separately, and then compare your responses. This is an exercise for you to undertake during your engagement. (This is not an activity that is designed to keep you occupied during your honeymoon flight to Hawaii.)

1. Was your decision to get married made too quickly?
2. Are you too young to be getting married?
3. Are you getting married for the wrong reasons?
4. Do you have unrealistic expectations about married life?
5. Are you (or Chris) bringing too much baggage into the marriage (and we aren't talking about extra luggage on the flight to Hawaii)?

If you are following these guidelines for making intentional and intelligent decisions about whom you date and whom you choose for a spouse, you will have greatly increased your chances for a successful marriage. We want nothing less for you (or Chris.)

Why An Engagement Can Be Considered "Successful" Even If You Break It Off

No one wants to have a broken engagement, but that is much better than a failed marriage. Your engagement is a last opportunity to test the extent of your compatibility. If, during your engagement, you and Chris discover some irreconcilable differences between you, cancel (or at least postpone) the wedding. Oh, you might disappoint a mother and a caterer, but that is better than being stuck in a bad marriage. So, don't ever worry about breaking off your engagement. If you have discovered a reason that you and Chris can't (or shouldn't) be married to each other for a lifetime, your engagement was successful because it brought you to a point of understanding *before* the wedding.

CHAPTER 8

Working Together

I n the past few chapters we have discussed your relationships with the people who will be most meaningful to you: family, friends, and Chris. Those groups may be the people who are most important, but they probably won't be the groups with whom you spend the most time.

If you subtract the time you spend sleeping, about half of the time you have left is going to be divided among those special people, but the other 50 percent is going to be spent with the people at work.

That's right. Those co-workers get at least half of your time and most of your attention. And they get the best part of your time—the middle of the day part. Your family, friends, and Chris get stuck with the first part of the day (when your attitude and your appearance may be at their worst), and the last part of the day (when you are wiped out and ready to punch out anyone who bugs you).

You might be thinking that the best part of you gets "wasted" on the people that you care about the least. Well, don't think about it that way. Instead, consider that the best part of you needs to be displayed to the people who know you the least. Your family, friends, and Chris already like you (probably), and they will give you the benefit of the doubt if you are just having a bad day and could use an attitude adjustment. But if you are consistently short-tempered at work, you're likely to get a reputation as always being that way (not to mention being tagged with an insipid nickname like "grouchy pants"). Not only do your co-workers know you the least, but it's likely that you have the least in common with them. After all—

- You weren't raised by the same parents (like your siblings).
- You may not have shared beliefs and common interests (like your friends).
- You aren't romantically attracted to them (like you are to Chris).

You just work with them. That may be the total extent of what you have in common. In this chapter we will discuss what it takes to establish meaningful relationships with these people who know so little about you and with whom you have so little in common. You should welcome the opportunity to build such relationships because they may help you become a better person (while you're getting paid at the same time).

Looking at the World Through the Eyes of Your Co-Workers

When you look at your work surroundings, you may see a building with offices (or perhaps cubicles), desks, chairs, computers, and Post-it notes. To you, the workplace may be nothing more than a physical place. *Your* world doesn't revolve around this place because you have a life outside of the office. (After all, you've read the preceding seven chapters of this book, so you have a real life.) The same may not be true of your co-workers. The center of *their* world might be defined by their nine square feet of cubicle space and the people around them.

If you're going to have any success in relating to your fellow workers, you are going to have to understand how they view their world, which is likely to fall into one of the following three main categories:

It's Existential

For some of your fellow employees, their world in the office is an existential experience. These people tend to be individualists whose motto is "every person for oneself" (the gender-neutral translation of "every man for himself"). They tend to be loners who believe they must make it on their own, with no help from anyone else. They feel totally responsible for their personal success or failure. They are going to make it or break it on their own.

If you are trying to relate to these people, realize that they live a rather lonely existence (in the office culture, at least). Isolating themselves from any sense of cooperation or camaraderie, they labor in relative solitude. These people often face despair at the prospect of trying to single-handedly overcome the responsibilities an employer expects a group of employees to shoulder. (You might see bumper stickers on their cars that read: "Life is hard. Then you die.")

The existential type is mired in misery, so don't expect this person to accept your cheerfulness or your offers of assistance eagerly. Existentialists tolerate loneliness and despair because that is all they expect from life. Don't be surprised if they reject your repeated attempts to bring a little brightness into their otherwise drab world.

Does this mean you shouldn't invite an existentialist to join in the birthday celebration for a fellow employee? It might be tempting, because they'll surely complain about the dry birthday cake or those lousy little plastic forks that break every time you take a bite. Let's face it. The existentialist is like Eeyore from Winnie the Pooh—sighing and moaning without ever having a positive thing to say. But don't give up. The existentialist needs to know that there is hope beyond oneself—a hope that can come from meaningful relationships with other people and with God. They can start to get a glimpse of such hope when they come in contact with you.

It's All Relative

We live in a time that philosophers and sociologists refer to as postmodernism: Everything is relative, and there is no absolute truth. The relativists in your office think that whatever degree of morality works for you is fine *for you*, but their own morality will do just fine for them. The rule of relativism is that there are no rules. Each person gets to define acceptable behavior according to his or her own standard. We like to call it "gastrointestinal morality"—you determine what is right or wrong for you based on your "gut" instincts. (And hopefully, you won't have Mexican food for lunch or else your standards of acceptable behavior may get really bizarre during the afternoon.)

If you happen to follow biblical principles, you're likely to have some interesting discussions with the relativists who work beside you. They won't mind that you use the Bible as a standard in your life, but they'll strongly object to any notion that the Bible should be used as a benchmark for *their* conduct.

Don't let this difference of opinion discourage you from befriending them. Their opinion makes as much sense to them as yours does to you, so respect their personal beliefs even though you don't agree. Over time, they might realize that your fixed positions (derived from a God who never changes) give you a solid foundation for your life and relationships—something that their life lacks because their foundation is constantly swaying with each cultural shift.

It's All About Money

A third group viewpoint that you're likely to find at work focuses on materialism. These are the people for whom wealth and possessions serve as the benchmark for success and happiness. They have the license plate frames that read: "The one with the most toys wins."

Because of the insidious peer pressure of others just like them, the materialists get caught up in a vicious cycle of acquiring more and more stuff. With each acquisition they make, the acceptable minimum level is raised up a notch. It creates a type of competition within the office for who can have the first, or the biggest, or the most expensive of whatever is the current fad of the affluent. This philosophy can easily pervade an entire office as fewer and fewer people receive a sense of personal satisfaction from their work and, instead, labor solely for the sake of money without regard for the significance of their responsibilities.

If you have managed to find contentment in your circumstances (because your sense of well-being stems from your address book instead of your bankbook), you have a lot to offer the materialists in your office. They are likely to be under continual stress with worries about the things they own or want to acquire (not to mention the debt they've accumulated to acquire the things). You can provide them with a vivid contrast of lifestyle. This is not to say that you must forsake all brand name apparel and accoutrements. (It's hard to hide the "Tommy Hilfiger" label emblazoned in three-inch letters across your pullover cardigan.) But you can show them that your satisfaction with life is not dependent upon your possessions. (And that fact will be obvious to any observer who sees your self-assured attitude in the office and your 1987 Yugo in the parking lot.)

People are funny.
They spend money they don't have
to buy things they don't need
to impress people they don't like.

Your Attitude: On-the-Job Asset or Occupational Hazard?

If you don't care about establishing meaningful relationships with people at work, you can have any attitude you want. Your life will be more enjoyable, however, (and your potential for advancement within the company enhanced) if you display an attitude that fosters cooperation and harmony among the troops. In other words, even if you don't care about the others, have a good attitude. It's in your own best interest.

It isn't always easy to maintain the best of attitudes in the middle of work pressures. The time demands of the job, the implicit competition between employees vying for limited advancement opportunities, and the dynamics of interpersonal relationships can bring out the worst in you (or if not the *worst*, then at least a side of you that's not too pretty). Perhaps you'll find it helpful to review some of the most common ugly attitudes that might creep out of you if you aren't paying attention. Any one of these can be particularly detrimental to your relationships at work.

1. Unbridled Ambition. Ambition can be an admirable trait, and you can be sure that most employers will reward your extra efforts if you are a self-starter and a hard worker. But *unbridled* ambition can be destructive and divisive. Your ambition is out of control when you don't care if you trample anyone who gets in your way. Make sure that your personal initiative does not leave the corpses of fellow employees in the office corridor. It's better to tone down your momentum than to misuse and abuse your co-workers in your attempts to rack up accomplishments.

Abuses of Power

If you are in a position of authority, you are particularly vulnerable to running roughshod over the feelings of other employees. In dealing with subordinates, you must be particularly sensitive to how your actions are perceived. They already resent you because you have the corner office while they are stuck at a TV tray by the photocopy machine. Take extra care to deal fairly with them.

In his book *The Empowered Leader*, Professor Calvin Miller identifies several telltale signs that might indicate you are abusing your power over subordinates:

- Giving up disciplines that you still demand from subordinates
- Believing that others owe you whatever you demand of them
- Trying to smooth things over rather than make things right
- Closing your mind to every suggestion that you yourself could be out of line
- Believing that people in your way are expendable

---

2. Greed. Relationships are jeopardized when dollars have a higher priority than people. Don't get so wrapped up in meeting deadlines, surpassing sales projections, and beating the budget that you sacrifice people in the process.

3. Gossip. Nothing will undermine your relationships faster than spreading gossip about your co-workers. Most people refuse to admit that their idle chatter constitutes gossip. But that is exactly what information is if it's about someone else and not complimentary. Gossip usually takes the form of belittling someone else in a way that makes you seem superior. You will actually strengthen your workforce and your work relationships if you refuse to get dragged into a gossip session.

> ### The best thing to do behind a person's back
> ### is to pat it.

4. Pride. Pride can be an admirable trait when it motivates you to do your best. But it can be destructive when self-centeredness alienates other people. Pride can keep you from admitting your mistakes and refusing to accept the legitimate contributions and suggestions of others. Never allow yourself to reach a point where you are unable to swallow your pride without choking.

5. Laziness. Few things are worse on the job than someone who is lazy. The employee who is a sluggard displays disrespect for every diligent worker in the division. If the people who work for you don't respect you, then it is impossible to have a meaningful relationship with them. While they may be outwardly cordial to you (because they know who signs their paychecks), they will inwardly despise you.

> ### You won't get ahead by taking credit
> ### for all the hard work that somebody else does.

Familiarity Breeds Romance

At the beginning of this chapter, we suggested that you might not have much in common with your co-workers because you are not romantically attracted to them. That may not be universally true. In fact, there may be an "office romance" in your future. Hey, there may be an office romance in your present. Think about it. If you are spending sixty to eighty hours per week on the job, you don't have the time or energy to go anywhere else to meet someone. Because romance, or the prospect of it, may keep you from thinking clearly, let us remind you of a few things that you might be inclined to forget (or ignore):
  • If you are the boss, don't get involved in an office romance. If the relation-

(continued on next page)

ship breaks up, one of Bruce's sleazy lawyer friends will be suing you for sexual harassment (for which Bruce will be asking for a nice fat referral fee). And if the relationship doesn't break up, then some other disgruntled employees will get a lawyer and sue you on some cockamamie claim that they were passed over for advancement because you were promoting your snuggle-bunny. Either way, you lose big and Bruce gets a referral fee.

- If you are dating your boss, you've got to question his or her judgment. If the relationship has serious potential, you might want to consider changing jobs so the interpersonal relationships of your co-workers aren't a problem.
- Don't think that you can keep the relationship a secret from the other people at work. That little love note you E-mailed is likely to be discovered and posted on the office Intranet.

The Courtesy of Confrontation

As you work side by side with people, situations are bound to arise when you will have to confront someone. Many people fear confrontation and avoid it at all costs. This is usually a big mistake—problems don't usually get better by themselves; they usually get worse.

Suppose that a person's behavior on the job has been inappropriate. If this situation is ignored:

- Your company suffers from a loss of morale in its employees;
- The individual suffers because he isn't given an opportunity to learn from his mistakes; and
- Everyone else suffers because they have to endure the continuing inappropriate behavior.

If it becomes your job to confront the offender, then you may want to consider these guidelines so that your dialogue can be productive instead of explosive:

✔ *Confrontation Rule #1: Do it as soon as possible.* These matters don't get better if they are left alone. The confrontation is best if it occurs close to the time the offensive action occurred.

✔ *Confrontation Rule #2: Do it privately.* Don't make a public display of the process. The offender is likely to act defensively if there is an audience. Be as discrete as possible in order to protect the offender's dignity (of which there may be little left).

✔ *Confrontation Rule #3: Identify the problem specifically.* Before you begin, make sure you have rehearsed what you are going to say. You must be able to articulate the offending action and why it was wrong (if that isn't obvious).

✔ *Confrontation Rule #4: Be more concerned about the individual than the problem.* Make sure you are critical of the action, not the person. You want to eliminate the problem and preserve the person. (Don't get things mixed up and think that you are supposed to eliminate the person.)

Exhibit Leadership Qualities (Even If You Aren't a Leader Yet)

Why do people follow a leader? Often it is because the leader has character traits that are attractive to people. Don't think that you have to be given a promotion at work before you have an opportunity to let your leadership qualities shine. Here are a few key leadership qualities that you can exhibit on the job right now.

1. Be confident and modest.
2. Be a good listener.
3. Be an encourager.
4. Be a problem solver.
5. Be quick to change your opinion but not your values.
6. Be a good example.

Servant Leadership Goes for the Towel, Not the Title

As discussed in the preceding section, leadership is an essential skill in the workplace, and you should attempt to exhibit leadership qualities even if you don't have a fancy title or a nameplate on a door (or even if you don't have your own office door). Much of leadership involves the relational aspects of dealing with people. This is an important skill whether you are working as a leader in the group or as a member of the group.

Modern leadership theory recognizes a principle called "servant leadership." The principle was articulated thirty years ago by John Greenleaf (considered the guru of leadership). We find it curious that so much praise and attention has been heaped upon Greenleaf for his "revolutionary insights" of servant leadership. To our way of thinking, Greenleaf just identified what Jesus actually displayed about two thousand years ago.

Jesus Christ is universally recognized as history's greatest servant leader. The episodes of his life give plenty of examples for learning how to relate to other people. One incident is particularly instructive for learning how to react as a servant leader. In John 13, the story is told of Jesus, who on the night before he was crucified, went to the Upper Room with the disciples. The men had been walking on the dusty roads of Jerusalem all day, and their feet were dirty. At that time it was customary for a servant to wash the feet of dinner guests, but there was no one available to wash the disciples' feet when they sat down for dinner.

While the disciples were engaged in conversation (probably arguing about which of them was Christ's favorite), Jesus grabbed a towel, poured water into a basin, and began washing the feet of the disciples. Look at what this single act can teach you about serving others as a leader:

- **A servant leader sees the need (maybe before anyone else does).** We're not talking about what already needs to be done or what is already included in your job description. Jesus did the foot washing voluntarily. It wasn't required of him, it just needed to be done.

  Maybe you say: "Those kinds of things never occur to me." Well, it didn't occur to the disciples, either (they were too preoccupied with themselves). That's what makes servant leadership so unusual. Servant leaders think about the needs of others above their own.

- **A servant leader responds in humility.** Jesus didn't make a big deal about what he was doing. He didn't insist on recognition. He just did the job. Of all the people in the room, he should have been the last person to be given this task, but he didn't try to pawn it off on someone else. He didn't say, "This isn't my job," or, "This is beneath me," or, "I'm too important to be doing this." Jesus displayed the heart of a servant leader, a heart that never says, "I'm saving myself for the important stuff, so I'll leave these menial jobs to someone else."

- **A servant leader shows no favoritism.** Don't overlook the fact that Jesus washed the feet of Judas, even though Jesus knew that this man would betray him in a few hours. (If it had been us, we think we would have twisted a few of the traitor's toes until the toe knuckles popped out of their sockets.)

  What an amazing lesson for servant leaders. We should be serving even those who don't like us. We should be serving others even when we know it won't be appreciated. We should be willing to serve our enemies.

- **A servant leader takes action.** It is not enough to see a problem, to understand what needs to be done, and to be available to take some action. After Jesus started the foot washing, each of the disciples saw the need and knew what needed to be done. But only Jesus put physical effort into making it happen. Seeing the problem and knowing about it are irrelevant factors unless you are willing to step up and take some action.

If you are looking to establish meaningful relationships where you work, start being a servant leader. People will be attracted to you when you are more concerned with using the towel than claiming a title.

Society defines a successful person as someone who rises above the crowd and rules over them. Servant leadership, as demonstrated by Jesus Christ, defines a successful person as someone who bends down to serve others.

Who You Are Is As Important As What You Do

From your employer's perspective, you are hired to fulfill a function. You have an assigned role in the organization, and you should give yourself wholeheartedly to that task. But don't think that your company cares only about *what* you do. Every good employer knows that *what* you do is not ultimately as important as *who* you are.

You may be able to perform your task with a high degree of technical skill, but if your personality is so abrasive that they have to build a "cone of silence" around you, then you are more disruptive than you are valuable. Conversely, if you can perform the technical tasks at an acceptable level but excel in building morale, you are more valuable than any piece of sophisticated machinery (except perhaps the vending machine in the lunchroom; workers would revolt without it).

- Pay attention to how you perform your job. You won't have a job if you don't do it well.
- But also pay attention to the kind of person you are. Your positive attitude and personality can't be replaced by advancements in technology.

It's More Than Just a Job

Your company isn't running a popularity contest. We aren't trying to give you advice that will allow you to "win friends and influence people" for the purpose of climbing the corporate ladder of success. Our intent is to challenge your concept of what you do at work.

Most people consider their job to be just that: a job, something to earn a buck (actually, sixty-seven cents after withholding). What a shame. With all the time you spend at the job, you should have more to show for it than two quarters, a dime, one nickel, and two pennies (which is sixty-seven cents for those of you who only use debit cards and have forgotten about coins and currency).

We want to challenge you to consider your job to be more than a workplace. Consider it your opportunity to positively impact the lives of the people who work with you. You don't have to make every co-worker your best friend, but you should be friendly to each of them. There are several steps you can take to change your perspective in this manner:

• ***Be more concerned about your responsibilities than about your rights.*** Of course, this is not the natural order of things. Usually, people are worried only about their rights. They whine and complain that they should be getting higher pay, shorter hours, longer breaks, and better benefits. Be a contrarian. Instead of complaining, look for ways that you can bring a positive attitude into the company (and everyone will be wondering what you're up to).

• ***Be a moral influence in the workplace.*** You probably don't have to look closely to notice that your co-workers are cheating the company. Maybe they are cheating on time cards, or charging personal long distance calls to the company, or trying to sneak out with a fax machine tucked in their pants. Don't fall into the trap of doing what you know is wrong just because "everyone does it." Stick to your personal ethical standards. (After all, how often do you need to send a fax from your pants?)

• ***Be an agent for reconciliation, not a source of disruption.*** If you have followed the steps we have outlined above, you will be a respected member of the workforce (regardless of whether you are management or just one of the worker bees). When you have a reputation for being a person of integrity, you will have a great deal of influence. Use your influence wisely and for the common good. Seek to reconcile parties who are at odds with each other. This will enhance the environment for everyone. Avoid the temptation to use your influence to create dissention.

From Workplace to Battlefield:
Dealing With Difficult People

We hope that the discussion in this chapter gives you some practical advice that will allow you to establish some meaningful relationships where you work. But regardless of how friendly you are, you are bound to run into a few people who will make your life difficult. But it won't happen only at work. These "difficult people" will confront you everywhere. (Not the same people in every place. They spread out so they can pop up everywhere that you go.)

In the next chapter, we'll talk about how you can get along with (or at least refrain from strangling) those people who seem to be your nemeses.

CHAPTER 9

Dealing With Difficult People

Wouldn't it be nice if everyone else in the world were just like you—your pleasant personality, your charm, your generous nature, your easygoing disposition, and your incredible sense of humor?

Just think of the possibilities! All conflict as we know it between people and nations would cease. Poverty would end, and prosperity would increase. People would be interesting, and politicians would be honest. No more demanding bosses, no more rude telemarketers, and no more incompetent workers. It would be a perfect world ... if everyone else in the world were just like you.

Yeah, right.

Actually, what we've just described is more like your worst nightmare than your greatest dream. Can you imagine a world with nothing but *you* in it? Hey, we tried (and since we don't know you, we imagined a world with people just like us, and it was really scary).

Even if the world were full of people who had only your positive personality traits, the best you could say is that it would be boring. But what if your clones consistently exhibited your more negative tendencies? Now we're talking the end of the world as we know it.

OK, so our little fantasy is never going to happen, but we hope this mental exercise has prompted you to begin thinking about the topic of this chapter—*you*.

"Wait a minute," you burst out incredulously. "I thought this was a chapter about difficult people!"

Precisely.

Difficulties and Differences

Each of us, at some time and in different ways, is a difficult person. Some aspect of our personalities is bound to rub someone the wrong way. Of course, we always think it's other people who are difficult, not us. It's always their problem, not ours.

To illustrate our point, let's say we were to ask you to make a list of characteristics you find difficult in other people. Your hit parade of personality types would probably include some of the following descriptions:

Bossy	**Negative**
Impatient	**Dishonest**
Manipulative	**Moody**
Quick-tempered	**Critical**
Know-it-all	**Unforgiving**
Exaggerates	**Indecisive**
Hard to please	**Too compromising**
Restless	**Lazy**
Undisciplined	**Worried**
Talks too much	**Discourages**

Now, let's say we were to ask you to make a list of your own annoying habits. What is it about *you* that could make you hard to deal with at times? Would your list look anything like this?

Assertive	Realistic
Impulsive	Clever
Too protective	Colorful
Overreactive	Overly helpful
Too confident	Good memory to a fault
Stretches the truth	Careful with decisions
Self-image is too strong	Pleaser
Fidgety	Too relaxed
Free spirit	Plans too much
Verbose	Not encouraging enough

Now look at the two lists. See what we've done? Same characteristics—listed two different ways. The first way is the way you might see others (these are personality disorders), and the other is how you might see yourself (now they are colorful traits).

When dealing with difficult people, understand that you are dealing with people who are essentially just like you—not in their personalities, but in their tendency to view others more critically than themselves. All of us tend to see others in a more critical light than we should, while we see ourselves more favorably than we should. This is a very important principle to understand as you build your relationship network, regardless if you are dealing with family members, friends, co-workers, neighbors, or even enemies. We like to call this principle:

Bruce & Stan's Second Law of Relationships

As we connect with people, we tend to be more critical of the faults we see in them than the faults we see in ourselves, even if they are the same faults.

We can't claim credit for this particular law. Jesus beat us to the punch when he told this story about a little speck of sawdust and a big old log.

> And why worry about a speck in your friend's eye when you have a log in your own? How can you think of saying, "Friend, let me help you get rid of that speck in your eye," when you can't see past the log in your own eye? Hypocrite! First get rid of the log from your own eye; then perhaps you will see well enough to deal with the speck in your friend's eye.
>
> LUKE 6:41-42

Yes, there are difficult people in the world, but most of the time the people you connect with every day aren't *difficult* as much as they are *different*. We would be a lot less impatient if we would try to see them as people with unique gifts and abilities. We would get less frustrated with "difficult" people if we saw their difficulties as positive qualities rather than negative traits. Remember our little scenario about everyone in the world being just like you?

"What If Your Body Was Just One Big Ear?"

A world full of people just like you would be like a body with just one big body part. The apostle Paul built his argument for the value of diversity in the church (also called the body of Christ) around this concept in his letter to the Christians at Corinth. He said that we need each of our body parts working together in order for the whole body to function.

> Suppose the whole body were an eye—then how would you hear? Or if your whole body were just one big ear, how could you smell anything?
>
> 1 CORINTHIANS 12:17

The body isn't built that way because that's not the way God designed it. God also designed the church so it would function effectively only when the various members—each with different strengths and weaknesses—work together.

The same principle applies to the world at large, including all of our relationships. God designed each of us to be unique as snowflakes (although we last a bit longer). The world needs us all—and you need a diverse bunch of people in your relationship network—whether we recognize it or not.

Defining Differences

Way back in 400 B.C., Hippocrates (yes, the guy who invented medicine) recognized four distinct personality traits and put them into four categories: choleric, sanguine, phlegmatic, and melancholic (hey, we're not crazy about the names, but that's what he called them).

Those terms may or may not look familiar to you. If they do, either you are a descendent of Hippocrates, or you have read Dr. Tim LaHaye's book *Transformed Temperaments*, in which he analyzes those four traits and offers sound biblical principles on how to maximize your strengths while minimizing your weaknesses. If you aren't familiar with the terms, here's a basic rundown. See if you can find yourself in one of the categories:

Personality	Description	Positive Qualities
Choleric	Driver	Decisive, confident, born leader, motivator
Sanguine	Expressive	Enthusiastic, creative, energetic, cheerful
Melancholic	Analytical	Thoughtful, organized, persistent, detailed
Phlegmatic	Amiable	Loyal, easygoing, kind, steady, patient

Gary Smalley has developed another way of describing these four personality types. He uses animals for each category (now there's something we can relate to!). See if you can't relate to one of these critters:

Personality	Animal	Equivalent Descriptor
Choleric	Lion	"The King of the Jungle"
Sanguine	Otter	"Party Waiting to Happen"
Melancholic	Beaver	"Always Busy"
Phlegmatic	Golden Retriever	"Man's (or Woman's) Best Friend"

Each of these four personality types has both strengths and weaknesses. In her book *How to Get Along With Difficult People*, Florence Littauer lists these:

Personality	Description	Weaknesses
Choleric	Driver (Lion)	Bossy, impatient, manipulative, quick-tempered, know-it-all
Sanguine	Expressive (Otter)	Prone to exaggerate, restless, undisciplined, talks too much
Melancholic	Analytical (Beaver)	Negative, hard to please, critical moody, unforgiving
Phlegmatic	Amiable (Golden Retriever)	Indecisive, too compromising, lazy, worried, prone to discouragement

Do these weaknesses sound familiar? They should. We listed them a few pages back as those traits you might find in difficult people. Can you see that these "weaknesses" or "difficulties" are found in all people? Obviously, no one person has all of these negative traits (except for your cousin Delbert). What you have are weaknesses that cluster around your predominant personality—

along with the complementary strengths.

As you mature and learn how to relate to people better, you are going to learn how to "accentuate the positive" while you "eliminate the negative" (and please, no more "Mr. In Between").

Handling Difficulties

As you build your relationship network, you're going to find that you will gravitate toward positive people whose strengths complement your weaknesses. But you are still going to run into difficult people, so you might as well learn to deal with them.

We like Florence Littauer's suggestions on how to handle difficult people. Her eight points are practical, and they all begin with the letter "C," which makes them easy to remember.

- *Compliment.* Every person, even the most difficult, has positive qualities. Resist the urge to be sarcastic and make it a point to find something good in everyone you meet. You'll be amazed at how people respond to genuine positive reinforcement.

- *Concern.* Sometimes difficult people are difficult because they have some real needs. Showing concern for someone means really listening and expressing a willingness to help. You aren't afraid to be a real friend.

- *Congratulate.* A compliment focuses on a personality trait, while congratulations target achievements. You may have to look for opportunities to express your congratulations, especially with someone you consider difficult, but the results will be well worth the effort.

- *Compromise.* To reach a compromise with someone doesn't mean you lose or give up something. It means you are a skilled relationship builder. When you compromise with someone, you take the best of what you have to offer and combine it with the best the other person has to offer.

- *Choice.* Nobody likes to be told what to do. We would all rather have a choice among two or more options. A smart relationship builder offers options rather than forcing other people into a corner.

- *Challenge.* Some people are difficult because no one has ever challenged them to be better than they are, or to achieve more than they have.

- *Confidence.* Do you ever wonder how "losers" get to be losers? Because people keep calling them losers! The way to build confidence in other people is to show concern, find their strengths, compliment them, and then congratulate them for a great job.
- *Conclusion.* Florence Littauer points out that our tendency is to want others to fill our needs rather than the other way around. As long as we continue to use people for our needs, we're going to find them difficult. Worse, other people are going to find us difficult! What we have to conclude is this: the only way to be fulfilled is to fulfill the needs of others.

**If you wish to be a success
And do all that you are able
Find someone in need of a chair
And seat them at the head of the table.**

Florence Littauer

What About the Really Difficult People?

The eight "C's" will be effective for 99 percent of the so-called difficult people you meet, because those people are just like you—only different! But what about those *really* difficult people? We're talking about people who are *negative, judgmental,* or *depressed.*

- *Negative* people seem like they were dropped on their heads as children, or at least weaned on a pickle. They are "the-glass-is-half-empty" people who never fail to snatch defeat from the jaws of victory. In general, we would advise you to steer clear of chronically negative people; you may not have the energy or stamina or the skills to correct their behavior. Worse, their negativity may influence you to be, well, negative.

    If you're up to the challenge (or are in a situation where you can't really avoid this person), then we advise you to be as positive and upbeat as you can. Counter their negative statements with positive ones. When they criticize someone, offer a compliment. Negative people will either change when they are around you, or leave you in search of negative reinforcement.

- *Judgmental* people start out negative and then blame other people for their problems. They are legalistic—meaning they interpret everything by the "letter of the law." And they let other people know just how wrong they are, how far they fall short of the perfect standard. Jesus didn't spend time around judgmental people, so we can't think of any reason why you should. Just make sure you check your own personality for any signs of a judgmental or legalistic attitude.

- *Depressed* people start out negative, move on to judgmental (where they blame others for their problems), and then end up depressed (where they blame themselves for their problems). They often play the role of the martyr and let everyone know how depressed they are. People with depression need professional help, but that doesn't mean you should give up on them. Be willing to be a real friend, but don't get caught in counseling situations where you are in over your head. Leave that to the experts.

Dealing With Enemies

A difficult person is someone you clash with; an enemy is someone who opposes you. A difficult person can be a pain, but an enemy is an adversary. If you have a lot of enemies, you are either a politician or a hunted criminal (sometimes those are the same person).

He who has a thousand friends has not one to spare,
And he who has one enemy will meet him everywhere.

Ralph Waldo Emerson

Truthfully, if you are a normal, red-blooded, law-abiding citizen—and you're not running for public office—then you probably don't have many enemies, and it's unlikely you're going to collect a bunch in your lifetime. Nonetheless, it is important for you to understand how to deal with your enemies, even if you don't think you have any. As we see it, there are three different categories of enemies.

1. People Who Oppose You. The people in this category include the class bully in the third grade who called you names and stuck his finger in your bologna sandwich. It may not seem like such a big deal now, but back then, a bully was a huge enemy. You could also put the high school adversary who deliberately smeared your reputation into this category. And then there's the whole matter of litigation, which pits people against each other. If you've ever been sued, you know what it feels like to have an enemy.

With these few exceptions, most of us don't keep our enemies very long. The bullies come and go, the smear tactics eventually stop, and lawsuits get settled. But what if you had an enemy who constantly opposed and even hated you?

It's interesting that Jesus talked to his disciples about this kind of enemy. The Gospel of Luke records a conversation between Jesus and his followers in which he gave them specific advice and encouragement on the subject of enemies. Here's what Jesus said:

> But if you are willing to listen, I say, love your enemies. Do good to those who hate you. Pray for the happiness of those who curse you. Pray for those who hurt you.
>
> LUKE 6:27-28

Jesus' words were prophetic; he knew that his followers were in for a very rough ride once Jesus was crucified. The Bible and history tell us that up until the events surrounding the death of Christ, Jesus' group of followers was fairly small and kept a low profile. But once people started converting to Christ in large numbers following his resurrection, the enemies of Christ came out of the woodwork.

You see, the teachings of Christ, upon which Christianity is built, were an offense to both the Roman Empire (which worshipped the emperor as a god) and to the religious leaders (who worshipped the law). These enemies thought they could kill the message (the Good News) when they killed the messenger (Jesus Christ). Little did they know the message would explode and expand like wildfire. So the enemies of Christ began a campaign of opposition fueled by hate against the followers of Christ. In effect, the enemies of Christ became the enemies of Christians. Of course, Jesus knew this when he said:

When the world hates you, remember it hated me before it hated you. The world would love you if you belonged to it, but you don't. I chose you to come out of the world, and so it hates you.

JOHN 15:18-19

Within sixty years of the crucifixion of Christ, all but one of Christ's original twelve disciples had been executed for their faith. Christians in the first century were murdered by the thousands as the "authorities" tried in vain to eradicate the memory and the message of Jesus.

Although we are twenty centuries removed from that bloody time, the persecution of Christians is alive and well today—maybe not in the Western hemisphere but certainly in some countries in Africa, Asia, and Eastern Europe. To those being persecuted for their faith in the twenty-first century, the words of Christ are as real and relevant today as they were when he first said them.

Why does Christ ask his followers to love those who hate, curse, and hurt them? Because—

- God is love (see 1 John 4:8).
- God sent Christ into the world out of his love for us (see 1 John 4:9-10).
- We need to love each other (see 1 John 4:11).

Christianity is nothing if it isn't based on love. Paul wrote that "there are three things that will endure—faith, hope, and love—and the greatest of these is love" (1 Corinthians 13:13). We believe in God through *faith;* our *hope* is in Jesus Christ and his resurrection; but unless we truly *love* others—including our enemies—our faith and hope can be called into question. Fred Smith wrote this in his book *You and Your Network:*

I believe God commands us to love our enemies because Christianity is a way of love and if we can love our enemies then we can love everyone. So long as there is anyone whom we cannot love, then our love is not complete. So long as we have not forgiven everyone, to that degree we cannot accept the forgiveness of God for ourselves. If we can love our enemies, then we have no difficulty believing God can love us.

"The One Guy You Don't Have to Love"

There is one enemy you don't have to love, and that's the devil himself. Satan is more than a cute guy in a red suit with horns and a pitchfork. He is a menacing evil presence (see Matthew 13:19), our adversary (see 2 Corinthians 11:14), a liar and a murderer (see John 8:44). In short, Satan is our enemy (see 1 Peter 5:8). The Bible instructs us to take a stand against him (see 1 Peter 5:9) and resist him (see James 4:7). The last thing we are to do is love him or anything he stands for.

---

2. People Who Offend You. Sometimes we turn other people into enemies because something they represent or stand for offends us. Unfortunately, this is common in three areas—race, religion, and politics. It's a sad and dark commentary on the human condition that most of the hatred people have for one another is generated by *racial, religious,* and *political* differences.

Racial differences. All we have to do is remind you about the Civil War and civil rights issues in America, the Holocaust in Europe, and the ethnic cleansing in Bosnia—and you know immediately that we have the capacity to make enemies of people who are different than us racially. The question you have to ask yourself is this: Is there any racial hatred in my heart? If there is—even a little—you need to bring it before the God who loves all people equally and with no discrimination (see Romans 10:12-13).

Religious Differences. All we have to do is bring up the destruction of Jerusalem and the dispersion of Israel in the first century, the Crusades in the Middle Ages, and the conflict between Protestants and Catholics in Northern Ireland in this century—and you know that we have the capacity to make enemies of those whose religion is different than ours. Christ told his followers to love their enemies, but we haven't always taken that teaching to heart. Look in your own heart and see if there is any hatred of those from other religions. Ask God to forgive you.

Political Differences. All we have to do is ask you to recall the horrors of the World Wars and all the other wars of this century—and you know without a doubt that people with political differences are capable of hating each other. Currently, we live in peace in our country, but what about your fellow citizens with "offensive" political or even moral beliefs? Do you hate them because you disagree with their political views or their personal lifestyles? A person's political views or lifestyle may be an offense to us, but we should never let that prevent us from loving the person. Jesus said:

> Stop judging others, and you will not be judged. Stop criticizing others, or it will come back on you. If you forgive others, you will be forgiven.
>
> LUKE 6:37

"We Are an Offense to God"

The next time you wonder if you should love and forgive someone who has offended you, think about this. In our natural state, we are an offense to God. In fact, because of the sin in our lives, we are the enemies of God. What if God had waited for us to become his friends before sending Jesus to die for us? We'd be in big trouble, because we aren't the ones who reached out to God. It was God who reached out to us "while we were still his enemies" (Romans 5:10).

---

3. People You Offend. There may come a time when you offend someone to the point of becoming his or her enemy. Not because of something dumb, like forgetting to wear deodorant. No, this is the kind of offense that comes from living "as children of God in a dark world full of crooked and perverse people" (Philippians 2:15). Those who are in the dark "hate the light because they want to sin in darkness" (John 3:20).

You don't have to condemn others for their dark behavior (and you shouldn't), but if you are living for Christ, you will undoubtedly be an offense to them.

Go for the Gold

A youth pastor recently told us about a high school student who invited God into his life. He was living with his mother, who was single but sleeping with various men. Without saying anything judgmental or condemning, the young man simply told his mother that he had become a Christian. His mother was so "offended" by his new relationship with God that she asked him to move out. The new Christian was deeply hurt, of course, but he understood that he was her "enemy" because of who he was, not because of something he had done. He forgave his mother and prayed that she would someday see the light of God's love.

This story illustrates what Jesus meant when he said:

> If someone slaps you on the cheek, turn the other cheek. If someone demands your coat, offer your shirt also. Give what you have to anyone who asks for it; and when things are taken away from you, don't try to get them back. Do for others as you would like them to do for you.
>
> LUKE 6:29-31

Do you recognize that last statement? It's commonly knows as the Golden Rule, and usually we recite it like it's some kind of happy saying meant to encourage us to do nice things for our friends. Far from it; the Golden Rule applies to our enemies. It applies to those who find us offensive because of Christ.

A Lifestyle of Love

The overriding principle in all your relationships needs to be love. This isn't just a good idea; it's God's command. Jesus said, "I command you to love each other in the same way that I love you" (John 15:12).

Loving others in the same way God loves us is no easy task. We need to ask God to fill us with his love so that we can truly love others, even when they disagree with us, and especially when they disagree with God. As we pray for the love of God to fill our lives, we need to remember that God doesn't ask us to love because he knows it will make us unhappy. Just the opposite is true: God asks us to love because he knows that our "joy will overflow" (John 15:11).

CHAPTER 10

Love Thy Neighbor

I t's not often that we get to talk about lawyers. Even though Bruce is a lawyer—and a good one at that—it's not something he likes to broadcast. When people find out Bruce is a practicing attorney, they either (a) can't wait to tell him a lawyer joke; (b) want some free legal advice; or (c) walk the other way. So we don't mention Bruce's profession all that often—except for now. In this chapter, we get to talk about lawyers. Well, actually only one lawyer, a particularly smart guy who lived two thousand years ago and had a conversation with Jesus Christ.

You may be wondering why we're bringing this particular character into our book about contacting and connecting with other people, especially now. Well, it just so happens that this lawyer asked one of the most significant questions ever—a question that goes to the heart of relationships and therefore to the heart of this book: *Who is my neighbor?* You'll recognize this story of the lawyer and Jesus. Here it is straight from the *New Living Translation* of the Bible:

One day an expert in religious law stood up to test Jesus by asking him this question: "Teacher, what must I do to receive eternal life?"

Jesus replied, "What does the law of Moses say? How do you read it?"

The man answered, "'You must love the Lord your God with all your heart, all your soul, all your strength, and all your mind.' And, 'Love your neighbor as yourself.'"

"Right!" Jesus told him. "Do this and you will live."

The man wanted to justify his actions, so he asked Jesus, "And who is my neighbor?"

Jesus replied with an illustration: "A Jewish man was traveling on a trip from Jerusalem to Jericho, and he was attacked by bandits. They stripped him of his clothes and money, beat him up, and left him half dead beside the road.

"By chance a Jewish priest came along; but when he saw the man lying there, he crossed to the other side of the road and passed him by. A Temple assistant walked over and looked at him lying there, but he also passed by on the other side.

"Then a despised Samaritan came along, and when he saw the man, he felt deep pity. Kneeling beside him, the Samaritan soothed his wounds with medicine and bandaged them. Then he put the man on his own donkey and took him to an inn, where he took care of him. The next day he handed the innkeeper two pieces of silver and told him to take care of the man. 'If this bill runs higher than that,' he said, 'I'll pay the difference the next time I am here.'

"Now which of these three would you say was a neighbor to the man who was attacked by bandits?" Jesus asked.

The man replied, "The one who showed him mercy."

Then Jesus said, "Yes, now go and do the same."

LUKE 10:25-37

Isn't that a great story? We all know it as the story of the Good Samaritan, a name that has become synonymous with doing good for others, particularly others in need of help. You've heard the story since you were a little kid, but you probably didn't know that it was a lawyer's questions that prompted Jesus to tell it.

The lawyer who questioned Jesus specialized in religious law. Because he was an expert, he didn't want information (he already knew the answer). Instead, he wanted to find out how Jesus would answer his question, which was, "What must I do to receive eternal life?"

Of course, being the smartest man who ever lived, Jesus turned the tables and asked the lawyer to answer his own question. The lawyer then correctly quoted what was written in the law. The first part of his answer came from Deuteronomy 6:5—

And you must love the Lord your God with all your heart, all your soul, and all your strength.

The second part came from Leviticus 19:18—

Never seek revenge or bear a grudge against anyone, but love your neighbor as yourself. I am the Lord.

On another occasion Jesus quoted these two Scriptures when a religious leader asked, "What is the most important commandment?" Jesus replied that the "first and greatest commandment" is to love God with everything you've got. But the second and "equally important" commandment is to "love your neighbor as yourself" (Matthew 22:37-39).

Jesus knew this, the lawyer knew this, and we know this. There's no disputing what it takes to obey God and "inherit eternal life" in the process: *Love God and love others.* What is open to dispute is how well we follow these commands. In other words, does our *walk* back up our *talk?*

Time to Walk the Talk

We may talk about loving God with our whole being, but do we really love him to the extent that we want to please him in everything we do? As we build our relationship network with friends and family and co-workers—and even our enemies—do we genuinely love these people?

"We Can't Do It Alone"

Loving God and loving others may seem like a simple task, but it's a tall order. Honestly, we can't do it on our own. We're just too self-centered. We're great at loving ourselves, but loving our Creator and our neighbor—now that's a different story.

It isn't enough just to know what is right. The Jewish priest and the Temple assistant knew the law better than anyone, so they knew the Jewish crime victim was their neighbor, and they knew what it meant to love him. But their own sin and self-centeredness prevented them from doing the right thing.

The same goes for us. We will do the right thing only when our lives are made new on the inside by the power of the Holy Spirit. When we control our lives, we get sinful and selfish results. "But when the Holy Spirit controls our lives, he will produce this kind of fruit: love, joy, peace, patience, kindness, goodness, faithfulness, gentleness, and self-control" (Galatians 5:22-23).

Everything We Need

The beauty of these two commands to love God and love others is that they contain everything we need to live our lives as children of God and citizens of this world.

- By loving and serving God we are taking care of the *vertical* relationship of our lives.
- By loving and serving others, we are taking care of the *horizontal* relationships of our lives.

If you were to illustrate this principle with a diagram, it would look something like this:

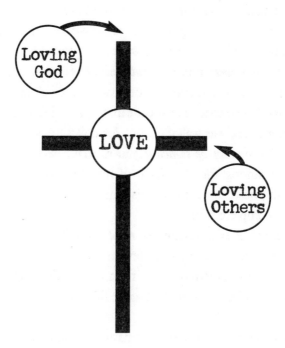

Notice that love is the key to both kinds of relationships. Love is the connector between us and God—and between us and everyone in our relationship network. Without love it is impossible to meaningfully connect with other people. More importantly, without love it is impossible to meaningfully connect with God.

Who Is My Neighbor?

Let's get back to the story of Jesus and the lawyer. After correctly answering his own question, the lawyer pressed Jesus further and asked, "And who is my neighbor?" You can't tell if this first-century barrister had a little smirk on his face when he asked this question (as if he were trying to trap Jesus), or whether he really didn't know. Perhaps he thought he knew the answer and merely wanted to see if Jesus would agree with him. In any case, we don't think he was expecting the answer Jesus gave, which was the story of the Good Samaritan.

What's amazing about the story of the Good Samaritan is that it tells us what it means to *have* a neighbor, as well as what it means to *be* a good neighbor. First, here's what it means to *have* a neighbor:

- *A neighbor doesn't have to live next door to you.* The poor guy who was robbed and beaten and left for dead was traveling a lonely and dangerous stretch of road. He wasn't in a house. He wasn't even in a neighborhood. He was walking from Jerusalem to Jericho.

- *A neighbor can be someone you've never met.* The unnamed traveler wasn't among friends. None of the three people who saw him—the Jewish priest, the Temple assistant, and the Samaritan—knew him. He was a complete stranger.

- *A neighbor is a person in need.* Nobody in the history of stories needed help more than the Jewish traveler. He wasn't just robbed. He was beaten and stripped and then left for dead. He had great physical needs, and he probably had some financial needs as well.

Second, the story of the Good Samaritan shows us what it means to be a good neighbor:

- *A Good Samaritan neighbor knows what it's like to be in need.* Notice how the Bible describes the Samaritan. It doesn't refer to him as "good," but rather "despised" (we still use the word "Good" to describe him, because the "Despised Samaritan" doesn't sound too appealing).

  Jews and Samaritans were like the Irish Protestants and Catholics of their day. They hated each other. The Jews thought they were better than the Samaritans, whom they considered to be "half-breeds"—with both Jewish and Gentile bloodlines. There's no question this traveling Samaritan knew what it was like to be in need. Maybe that's what prompted him to help this man, even though he belonged to the class of people who hated him.

- *A Good Samaritan neighbor goes out of his way to help a neighbor in need.* Notice that the Jewish priest and the Temple assistant went out of their way to avoid the crime victim, but the Samaritan went out of his way to help. From the Bible text, it's clear that the Samaritan was just as busy as the two religious officials. He was on a schedule and probably had appointments lined up, but he set everything aside to help the man in need, his neighbor. He was motivated by his compassion, not his self-interest.

- *A Good Samaritan neighbor makes personal sacrifices to help a neighbor in need.* The Samaritan didn't just say, "Wait here, I'll go down the road and find someone to help you." He took responsibility to personally help this stranger in need. He used his own supplies, tore his own coat to make bandages, put the bleeding man on his only mode of transportation, and then took him to the nearest inn. Through the night he tended to the beaten man's wounds, and then left money (the equivalent of two days' wages, enough for a few weeks in the inn) before continuing his journey the next day. He even agreed to cover any additional expenses.

The Good Samaritan was the stuff of which legends are made. When someone today does a Good Samaritan-type deed, we call him a hero. He makes headlines. He gets his own segment on the Fox television special, "The World's Most Amazing Neighbors." But we shouldn't look at the Good Samaritan as a hero. He's the kind of person Jesus wants us to imitate every day.

Wilson Is Not Your Neighbor

We've got this all backward. Rather than being a good neighbor to others, we're looking for neighbors who can do stuff for us. We all dream of having a neighbor like Wilson, the wise and mysterious neighbor of the Taylor family from "Home Improvement." Wilson may be a little eccentric, but we love him because he's never a bother, and he's always there when Tim needs him.

But Wilson is not a "good neighbor," because Wilson is a fantasy.

- A good neighbor is not the person who lives next door.
- A good neighbor is not the guy who keeps his yard neat and tidy and his house freshly painted.
- A good neighbor is not the family with the perfect kids who excel in school and sports, and who will watch your kids anytime you need a sitter.

- A good neighbor is not the good-looking guy in the apartment below yours who will repair your broken microwave at the drop of a hat.
- A good neighbor is not the brilliant day trader in your condo association who volunteers hot stock tips.

It would be great to have neighbors like these, but they aren't what Jesus was talking about, and they aren't what you should be looking for. It shouldn't be your goal in life to find neighbors who will enrich your life. God is calling you to something higher as you contact and connect with people. *He wants you to be a Good Samaritan neighbor to people in need.*

So who is your neighbor? We thought you'd never ask.

These Are Your Neighbors
The truth is, your neighbors come from these five groups of people:
- Your family
- Your friends
- Your spouse
- Your co-workers
- Your enemies

Gee, do these look familiar? They should. We've covered these five groups of people in Chapters 5-9. These are the people in your relationship network. These are your neighbors, and at some point in their lives, every one of them will be in need, just like you will be in need. No, they won't take turns lying in a ditch after getting robbed and beaten, but they will have real life problems, pressures, and predicaments, and you may be the person God uses to love them and have mercy on them like a Good Samaritan.

"Strangers in the Night"

What about strangers, those people you've never met? Are you supposed to be a Good Samaritan neighbor to every stranger who has a need? Of course not. There are so many people in the world and so many needs that it would be impossible for you to fill every one. You have a responsibility first and foremost to be a neighbor to those in your relationship network. But if God should put you in a position to help a stranger in need, you need to respond with Good Samaritan neighborliness. Besides, as the saying goes, a stranger is a friend you haven't met yet.

The Needs of Your Neighbors

The needs of the neighbors in your relationship network are going to be as varied and complex as their personalities and circumstances. We're not suggesting that you run around in a panic, trying to be a Good Samaritan to all people. You can't do it, and if you try, you're going to get so stressed and fatigued that before long, you will be the one with the greatest needs.

What we are going to do is give you a general overview of seven different categories of needs that people can have at any given time:

- relationship needs
- health needs
- financial needs
- the needs of abused people
- neighborhood needs
- world disasters needs
- death needs

Thanks to an excellent book, *Helping a Neighbor in Crisis*—edited by Lisa Barnes Lampman, president of Neighbors Who Care (*www.neighborswho-care.org*)—we can give you some basic information on the needs you'll run into and how you can help.

As you look through these seven categories, see which ones touch your heart. Again, you can't be a Good Samaritan neighbor in every area of need, but God may be calling you to devote yourself to one or two areas. Maybe your interest comes out of personal experience. What you're going to find is that you will be very helpful in some specific areas of need, and in the areas where you don't have much interest or experience, you can always connect your neighbors with people who do. Here are the seven categories of need.

1. Relationship Needs. Most likely you're going to encounter needs in this category more than any other. As you connect with the people in your relationship network, you are going to run into needs such as these:

- *Marriage troubles* – These could range from simple disputes to affairs to divorce.
- *Rebellious children* – If a family has kids, then there are kid challenges. Some rebellion is natural, other times it's more serious.
- *Issues of loneliness* – Family connections may not be the problem at all. You may know someone who is isolated from family and doesn't seem to have any friends.
- *Depression and discouragement* – Depression affects a lot of people, and you may not know it until you really get to know someone.

How can you be a Good Samaritan neighbor in these cases?
- Don't be judgmental, and don't stick your nose in where it doesn't belong.
- Be a good listener and keep things confidential.
- If asked to help, be willing to give it.
- Don't take sides.
- Be ready to suggest places where your neighbor can get help.
- Pray (see Psalm 146:8-9; Mark 10:14; 2 Corinthians 7:6; Hebrews 13:4).

2. Health Needs. Everyone has health needs at one time or another. These can run the gamut from simple illnesses to catastrophic challenges:

- *Temporary illness* – These are the easy ones, like the flu or a minor operation.
- *Chronic illness* – Some people suffer from ongoing health problems or recurring illness.

- *Sick or special needs children* – Many families face challenges with their kids, and when this occurs, the needs can be great.
- *Catastrophic illness or injury* – These are devastating illnesses or diseases like cancer, or a terrible accident that can strike anyone.

How can you be a Good Samaritan neighbor in these cases?
- Give love and support by physically being there. Make the calls and send the cards, but offer to help in person.
- Don't blame your sick neighbors for their illnesses. This may sound strange, but there are people who actually try to help by saying, "If you just repent of your sins, you'll be healed immediately."
- Don't blame God. A wrong message would be to tell someone that God has caused an illness or accident for a reason. God *allows* these things to come into our lives, but we should not blame him for their origin.
- Offer to provide meals, baby-sitting, and financial assistance.
- Recommend a support group or someone who's been through the same health issue.
- Pray (see Exodus 15:26).

3. Financial Needs. Here's an area everyone can relate to. It doesn't matter how much or how little money people have, they always have financial needs:
- *Loss of a job* – Even in a thriving economy, people can lose their jobs, which can be particularly devastating.
- *Financial loss* – Have you made a lot of money in the stock market? Not everyone is so fortunate. Some people invest in businesses, only to have them go sour.
- *Debt crisis* – There's nothing more burdensome than to be under a heavy load of debt, and many people are in this situation.
- *Poverty* – Many families just can't make ends meet. You don't have to live in rural Mississippi or the inner city of Chicago to live in poverty.

How can you be a Good Samaritan neighbor in these cases?
- Be quick to listen and slow to give advice. People with financial needs are often embarrassed, so don't pry.
- Be an encourager. Suggest ways your neighbor can seek financial counseling or assistance.

- Don't take pity, and don't be smug just because you don't have money problems. A financial crisis can hit anyone, anytime.
- If you've gone through a financial crisis yourself, share your personal experience.
- Ask your church to get involved. Some churches have programs and funds to temporarily help disadvantaged people.
- Pray (see Philemon 1:4-6).

"What Businesses Are Doing"

Statistics show that the income gap between the rich and the poor is widening. What the numbers don't reveal is that there is a growing trend among successful business people—especially those entrepreneurs who have made a lot of money in high-tech industries—to give back to their communities and help disadvantaged people. Some provide computer training, others give long-term loans for start-up businesses, and still others move their businesses and factories into transitional neighborhoods, providing jobs and opportunities for the residents.

---

4. The Needs of Abused People. There are two kinds of abuse: self-inflicted abuse and abuse inflicted by others. Both kinds are a growing problem in our society:

- *Alcoholism* – Alcohol abuse is often a mask for other problems, but it is also a growing problem among high school and college kids who succumb to pressure from their peers.
- *Drug abuse* – Just when we thought we had won the drug war, people find new drugs and new ways to use them.
- *Domestic violence* – Even Christians are not immune to this problem, which is usually inflicted by men on women and children.
- *Sexual abuse* – No one likes to talk about this insidious problem, but it is a reality, even in the church.

How can you be a Good Samaritan neighbor in these cases?

- Communicate your love and concern. Again, don't be judgmental, and listen with an open heart.
- Be direct and honest, especially where the abuse is self-inflicted.
- Encourage the abuser to be open with his or her family.
- Encourage the abuser to seek professional counseling.
- Encourage victims of abuse to seek professional counseling.
- Pray (see Psalm 107:13-16).

5. Neighborhood Needs. The needs of your neighbors can happen anywhere, but there are needs directly related to your actual neighborhood and community:

- *A natural disaster,* such as a fire, flood, hurricane, or tornado.
- *A one-on-one crime,* such as a robbery or burglary, can leave a victim feeling helpless and insecure.
- Many decent families in communities across the country live in *crime-infested neighborhoods.*
- *An outrageous neighbor* who causes problems for the whole neighborhood.

How can you be a Good Samaritan neighbor in these cases?

- Be patient. Recovering from personal or neighborhood disasters takes time.
- Listen for needs.
- Offer practical help, such as food, shelter, clothing, as well as financial assistance.
- Suggest a person or an agency that could intervene.
- Support inner-city ministries that help families in tough neighborhoods.
- Pray (see 1 John 3:17-18).

"A Tale of One City"

We live in Fresno, California, a city known over the last several years for one of the highest unemployment as well as one of the highest crime rates in the nation.

Rather than sitting back and watching things get worse, several community ministry leaders took it upon themselves to move into high-crime neighborhoods and work to provide job training, reconciliation services, child care—and simply to be good neighbors. With many churches, community leaders, and business people joining the effort, things are getting better in Fresno. Dozens of ministries and thousands of volunteers work together in a way that has become a model for cities everywhere.

6. World Disaster Needs. Floods, famine, earthquakes, and other incredible disasters that crush people in poor countries are a constant reality in our world. Sometimes you wonder what you can do when these things happen:

- *Catastrophic disasters* that leave thousands if not millions homeless.
- *Ongoing health issues,* such as AIDS and other diseases.
- *Starvation* in underdeveloped countries or nations torn by civil war.
- *War and ethnic cleansing,* which seem to be a constant theme in several parts of the globe.

How can you be a Good Samaritan neighbor in these cases?
- Investigate the needs and pinpoint those that particularly interest you.
- Find out what others are already doing to help.
- Contact an agency and offer your personal and financial assistance.
- If you have the time and the resources to travel, take a trip and become personally involved.
- Pray (see Psalm 57:1).

7. Death Needs. Every single person faces the issue of death. Sometimes it's a natural process, and other times it comes unexpectedly.
- *Death of a family member or friend.* This could be someone in the immediate family, extended family, or the family of a friend.

- *Death of a child.* Few things are as anguishing as the premature death of a child.
- *Suicide* is particularly difficult and hard to understand.

How can you be a Good Samaritan neighbor in these cases?

- Express your sympathy in appropriate ways.
- Be available to help.
- Visit the people who are grieving when the time is right.
- Listen for needs.
- Offer to handle everyday tasks, such as providing meals.
- Don't offer pat answers. Sometimes it's best to just listen.
- Pray (see 1 Corinthians 15:54-55).

Jesus, Our Supreme Example

If ever we needed motivation to be a Good Samaritan neighbor, we only have to look as far as Jesus. He is our supreme example. Like the Good Samaritan, Jesus was despised (see Isaiah 53:3). Like the fellow who was victimized, we are helpless and without hope. While we were helpless and hopeless, Jesus came to our rescue. Yet he did more than bandage our wounds. He took our pain and our suffering upon himself.

We can never duplicate the sacrifice Jesus made for us, but we can adopt his attitude as we show concern for our neighbors and share their burdens. "Your attitude should be the same that Christ Jesus had," the apostle Paul wrote. "Though he was God, he did not demand and cling to his rights as God. He made himself nothing; he took the humble position of a slave and appeared in human form. And in human form he obediently humbled himself even further by dying a criminal's death on a cross" (Philippians 2:5-8).

Do you want to live your life the way God wants you to? Then love him with all you've got, and love your neighbor as you love yourself. Do you want to follow the example of Jesus Christ? Then serve others with the attitude of Jesus and the actions of the Good Samaritan. Not only will your life make a difference for others, but it will take on the kind of meaning most people only dream about.

Part III

Your Real Life and God

If all we cared about was helping you design a better relationship network, we could end the book right here. This would be the epilogue, you would close the book, and we'd all go home happy. But we can't do that. We'd be doing you a disservice if we didn't cover one more area of vital importance to your real life. So we're going to return to something we first talked about in Chapter 3 and then brought up from time to time throughout the book. It's your relationship with God. That's what the last two chapters of this book are all about.

CHAPTER 11

The Meaning of
Your Real Life

T hroughout this book we have encouraged you to connect with others in a way that enriches your life and the lives of everyone around you. We don't want you to go out into the world without a game plan, because real life is a contact sport. Just like you can't play real sports without teammates, coaches, fans, and opponents, you can't play the game of real life without family, friends, mentors, and enemies. So we have been suggesting ways for you to deliberately and meaningfully contact and connect with people.

The people you relate to in your real life are incredibly important. The way you relate to them will determine how successful you are, and how fulfilling your life is. But unless you have a vital relationship with God, you will never experience the true meaning of real life. And you will never know what it's like to have complete and total fulfillment apart from anything you do for people, or anything they do for you.

The Problem With People

Oh, boy, here we go contradicting ourselves. We've just spent ten chapters encouraging you to connect with people, and now we're going to tell you that people are a problem. Well, that's not exactly right. People aren't the problem. The problem is that our relationships with people can get in the way of a vital relationship with God.

Even though God has called us to connect with people in meaningful ways (see Matthew 22:39; 1 John 4:7-8), it's possible to put people before God if our goal is to please and impress people rather than God. Rather than doing all we can so that God can "approve" us (2 Timothy 2:15), we work to win the approval and acceptance of our family, our friends, our co-workers, and even our enemies.

Which brings us to another big problem. How can we tell when people approve of and accept us? Ninety-nine percent of the time we know because they respond to our *performance*. You know all about performance, because you've been doing it all your life just to win the approval of others:

- When you were a toddler, you did your duty on the toilet just so your parents would *praise* you.
- When you were in school, you studied hard so your teachers would give you *good grades*.
- When you got involved in sports, your success was based on the number of *points* you could score or the *best time* you could clock.
- When you got your first job, you did what the boss said so you would get an outstanding *performance review* and that coveted *salary increase*.
- When you took your company public, you were hoping that people would *approve* of you by buying up your shares and driving up the price.
- When you began attending church, you did the right things so the congregation would *accept* you as a member.

The Problem With Performance

By the time we're adults, we are so used to meeting or exceeding the performance standards of the authority figures in our lives that we can't help but approach our everyday relationships the same way. In other words, whether we intend to or not, we approve and accept the people in our relationship network based on what they do for us—and how well. Conversely, we are aware that the approval and acceptance that people give us are pretty much based on what we do for them.

We don't mean that we give out literal grades, points, or raises to our family and friends—or that we want the same from them. We keep score mentally, with little mental checklists, either praising the people who perform for us or writing off and resenting the people who fail to live up to our expectations. We know from experience that people evaluate us in the same way.

So what do you do about this performance trap, especially when you know it affects your entire relationship network? One solution would be to adopt an "I could care less what other people think" attitude. Yes, you could do that, but then you would be joining the ranks of social dropouts, deviants, and misfits who populate our society (as well as its jails and prisons). People who don't care what others think (and act accordingly) usually have other issues they are dealing with, starting with a poor self-image and a general dislike of others.

In order to maintain social order and civility, it's important to meet certain acceptable standards of behavior and performance. We're not suggesting that you stop performing for the approval of others. What we are suggesting is that you don't make that approval the basis for the meaning of your real life. You need to anchor the purpose for your life to something much more reliable. You need to put your trust in God rather than your own performance.

Separated from God and his Word, people have only their abilities and the opinions of others on which to base their worth, and the circumstances around them ultimately control the way they feel about themselves.

Robert Magee

Dr. Robert Magee, the author of *The Search for Significance*, reminds us that God wants to bring us into a relationship with him, where there is no condemnation (see John 3:16-17). On the other end of the spectrum, Satan "continues to deceive people, including many Christians, who believe that the basis of their worth is their performance and their ability to please others." Magee has this nifty little equation he calls "Satan's lie"—

Self-Worth = Performance + Others' Opinions

It's easy to buy into "Satan's lie," even if you don't consider yourself a follower of Satan or even a bad person. All you have to do is rely on your own performance in order to win the approval of others and, in the process, hope like crazy that you will find the meaning of life. The alternative is to rely on God and seek his approval, and find the meaning of life in the process.

Even if you already have a relationship with God, you still need to make a conscious decision to find meaning through him. Although your eternal destiny in heaven is secure, you still may be struggling with your own performance while you're living every day here on earth. You're not alone. We've met a lot of people who are struggling to find fulfillment in their lives right now. Some of these people know God personally, and others are still searching.

Where Are You Now?

We don't know where you are in your spiritual quest, but we are fairly certain that you fall into one of these categories:

- *Mature Christian.* You have a long-standing relationship with God and you know a lot about him. You also know that the more you learn about God, the more you realize what you don't know. So you're eager to learn more!
- *Adolescent Christian.* Like a growing teenager, you are excited about your increasing spiritual maturity, but your Christian growth still feels a bit inconsistent. You want to grow in your faith, but you're not quite sure how to get there.
- *Newborn Christian.* You're a relatively new Christian, and you want as

much spiritual food as you can get. Maybe you bought this book to find out more about living your Christian life.

- *Fence-Sitter.* People have told you about God, and you've done your own investigation (this book is part of the process). You believe in God, but you're not sure about whether you want a personal relationship with him. You still have a lot of questions.
- *Seeker.* You feel a need to connect with a higher power in a spiritual sense, but you aren't convinced that the God of the Bible is the only option out there. Still, you can't disregard God completely. You're open to him, but you're also open to other spiritual forces.
- *Contra-Christian.* So far you have completely rejected the God of the Bible. You've decided to go it on your own. God may be for some people, but he's not for you. You're reading this book strictly for the advice on relationships. You skip over the God stuff.

Which category best describes you? If the fence divides those who have a personal relationship with God and those who don't, which side of the fence are you on? Maybe you aren't even in the pasture yet! That's OK. Keep reading. We're not going to try to "convince" you to connect with God personally. We simply want to lay out the options for you. Then it's up to you to make the choice.

If you have already decided that connecting with God is a good idea, then we encourage you to read on as well. It's always a good idea to review the basics of your faith and your relationship with God. You never know when someone is going to challenge the things you believe, or more likely, want you to explain why you're a Christian. The apostle Peter advises us to "always be ready to explain" our "Christian hope," and to do it in a "gentle and respectful way" (1 Peter 3:15-16).

The reality is that if you are a Christian, you have a different belief system than your non-Christian friends, family, co-workers, and neighbors. You live in a different world than they do. But that doesn't mean you are supposed to keep out of their world. Just the opposite! Be their friend, show them the love of Christ, who was known as the "friend of the worst sort of sinners" (Matthew 11:19).

Two Different Worlds

Regardless of which "world" you live in—a world without God or a world with God—it's important to know how you believe (it's also important to know how those in the other world believe), because all beliefs have consequences. We're not making a judgment here (and neither should you). We just want to lay out the facts.

Some people think that believing in God is merely a preference, and that it's possible to lead a good and productive and meaningful life with or without God in your life. OK, we'll grant you that there are a lot of successful people who don't claim any special relationship with God. They may even seem to be satisfied with their lives. But how do they answer the three great questions of life?

- Where did I come from?
- Why am I here?
- What happens when I die?

In other words, what is the meaning of their lives? They could say, "Listen, those questions don't matter to me. I'm only concerned with my life and my relationships here and now. I don't need God or any other Higher Power to tell me how to live my life."

If you take God out of the picture of your life, then all you are left with is the material world around you and the years you have to interact with that world and the people in it. In other words, all you have is you and your performance while you're alive.

A World Without God

This way of looking at the world is called *naturalism*, because nature is all that matters. There is nothing beyond what we can see, touch, taste, or smell. People who believe in naturalism have what we call a "secular worldview."

"Your Worldview Is Showing"

In our book *Bruce & Stan's Guide to God*, we define *worldview* as "a personal belief system that colors everything we do in one way or another. It determines how we behave, the choices we make, and often how we feel."

When you have a secular worldview, here's how you see the world:

- God is not in the picture.
- All things in the world, including man, began from nothing and evolved naturally.
- As the highest evolved being, man is the measure of all things and the ultimate authority.
- There is no absolute truth; personal choice is what's most important.
- The government is the highest "law," and government is in the best position to decide what's best for people in all areas.

Let's say you have this worldview. How would you answer our three questions that lead to the meaning of life?

- *Where did I come from?* You'd have to conclude that you came from nothing. The universe and everything in it somehow evolved from impersonal forces. The world wasn't created, and neither were you. It was all some kind of "cosmic accident."
- *Why am I here?* Now, there's a good question! If you were an accident, there really isn't any reason for your being here on earth. So it's up to you to make your life count. Yes, it's true that you came into being when two other cosmic accidents decided to engage in a purely biological exercise, leading to your physical birth. But the only thing you have in common with them is the same thing you have in common with all other members of the human species—your DNA. So you better make the most of what you have and what you can do while you're alive, because there's no larger purpose for your life.

- *What happens when I die?* This is an easy one. Since you came from nothing, then there's nothing after you die. Your answer to the question, "Is that all there is?" is, "Yes, that's all there is."

A World With God

This way of looking at the world is called *theism*, because it includes God (*theos* is the Greek word for *God*). People who believe in God have what we call a Christian worldview.

When you have a Christian worldview, here's how you see the world:

- God is the Creator of and the Supreme Being in the universe.
- God created all things, and created humans in his own image. Because human beings are created in the image of God, we have dignity and purpose.
- God's revealed absolute truth comes first, and we build our personal beliefs and choices around it.
- God has ordained government as a means of keeping order in an imperfect world.

Let's say you had this worldview. How would you answer our three questions that lead to the meaning of life?

- *Where did I come from?* You came from God, who made you in his image and has created in you an eternal soul. In your soul God has placed a longing for something bigger than you and beyond your experience, something that can only be filled by God himself. You realize that life has an eternal spiritual dimension far beyond what you can see, touch, taste, and smell.
- *Why am I here?* God created you to glorify him and to enjoy him forever. That's the main reason you are here. God has also put you here on earth to manage and enjoy his creation, which glorifies God and testifies to his existence. Finally, God has you here on earth to love and enjoy other people, especially the people in your relationship network. When you add these three dimensions of life together—glorifying and enjoying God, managing and enjoying his creation, and loving and enjoying other people—your life takes on tremendous meaning and purpose.

- *What happens when I die?* The choices you make for God and the people you love through God while you are alive on earth will make a difference for now and eternity. After you die, the eternal part of your being—your soul—will live on. If you have accepted God's plan for life with him after death, then you will spend eternity in heaven.

Christianity claims ... to tell you what the real universe is like. Its account of the universe may be true, or it may not, and once the question is really before you, then your natural inquisitiveness must make you want to know the answer. If Christianity is untrue, then no honest man will want to believe it, however helpful it might be; if it is true, every honest man will want to believe it, even if it gives him no help at all.

C.S. Lewis

But Can I Really Believe It?

As you talk to people in your relationship network, you may find some who think that if you believe in God, you aren't thinking clearly. They believe that the only rational choice is to believe that there isn't a personal Creator, and that life is what you make it.

Well, we take exception with that. If anything, there is more reason for you to believe in a personal God who created the universe than to believe that the universe created itself. In fact, if you are intellectually honest, and you investigate the facts about the universe and how it got here (as well as how it works), here's what you will conclude:

It takes more faith to believe the universe and everything in it (including you) is a cosmic accident than it does to believe that an intelligent Creator purposefully made the universe and everything in it (including you).

Forgive us if we're going over some basic stuff here, but this is critical to your thinking (in fact, they call this "critical thinking"), regardless of what side of the fence you're on or what world you're in. If you aren't convinced that God matters, give these next four points some thought. If you truly believe that God matters in your life and in the lives of the people you contact every day, then make sure you know these things cold. Like the Boy Scouts, always be prepared.

Four Arguments for the Existence of God

Since God is a Spirit, no one has actually seen him, but God has left us some strong evidence—you could call it "rational proof"—for his existence. Take a look at these basic arguments for the existence of God, which we first talked about in *Bruce & Stan's Guide to God*.

1. The Ontological Argument. The very fact that you have an idea of God points to his existence. Anthropologists agree that a belief in some kind of Supreme Being is found in every culture and every tribe on earth. Just as the earth's seas can't resist the gravity created by the moon, the human heart can't resist the tug of God.

> For the truth about God is known to them instinctively. God has put this knowledge in their hearts.
>
> ROMANS 1:19

2. The Cosmological Argument. Every effect must have a cause. You wouldn't walk up to a $200,000 Ferrari and say to the owner, "You know, this gorgeous car made itself. Oh, it took a long time, but over many years, the parts made themselves and came together perfectly."

How ridiculous! You take one look at the car and you know that someone built it.

And what about our universe? How could anyone believe that this incredibly complex system of planets and stars exploded from nothing, all by itself? What about the earth, which exists in perfect balance and harmony within our solar system, sustaining life for all of its living things? And what about your body, by far the most intricate and amazing machine in the universe? Are you going to buy into the notion that you evolved from some kind of primordial soup? No, all of these things we take for granted—the universe, the earth, our bodies—had a powerful cause or person to begin it. We believe that someone was God, the "First Cause."

> For every house has a builder, but God is the one who made everything.
>
> HEBREWS 3:4

3. The Teleological Argument. There is order, harmony, purpose, and intelligence in nature and the world. Logic suggests that an intelligent and purposeful being produced it. Take our Ferrari as an example. Not only do you know that someone built the car, but you can tell by looking at its beauty of form and function that some extremely gifted people designed it so everything would fit and work together.

Then look at the beauty of our world. The more you find out how beautiful, complex, and perfectly balanced the world is, the more you would expect that an intelligent and powerful Creator designed it all.

> From the time the world was created, people have seen the earth and sky and all that God made. They can clearly see his invisible qualities—his eternal power and divine nature. So they have no excuse whatsoever for not knowing God.
>
> ROMANS 1:20

4. The Moral Argument. One of the common characteristics of humans is that we have a moral code—a built-in sense of right and wrong. This has been true of every people and every civilization in recorded history. How could a moral compass—often called "the higher law"—just happen? This sense of right and wrong in the heart of every person is evidence of a moral Creator.

> They demonstrate that God's law is written within them, for their own consciences either accuse them or tell them they are doing what is right.
>
> ROMANS 2:15

There's One More Step

Even though these four arguments for the existence of God are compelling, they may not convince you beyond a reasonable doubt that God exists. That's OK. God isn't troubled by your doubts. (He exists quite nicely outside of your doubts, thank you very much.) You shouldn't be troubled by your doubts, either. God doesn't ask you to prove his existence. All he asks is that you believe by *faith* that what he has done for you is true and effective.

What has God done? Here it is clearly stated in the most famous verse in the Bible:

> For God so loved the world that he gave his only Son, so that everyone who believes in him will not perish but have eternal life.
>
> JOHN 3:16

The Choice Is Yours

Remember that we said we weren't going to try to "convince" you to connect with God personally? Neither is God.

God is the "perfect gentleman." God won't force himself on you: the choice is yours. You can decide either to accept Jesus Christ as God's only plan for your salvation (see Acts 4:12), or you can decide to live your life apart from God. The choice is yours.

Take Your Relationships to the Next Level

Now we're getting down to some "rubber meets the road" stuff. When you know God personally, he not only changes your life, but he changes the way you relate to other people. That's why we really believe this:

**Your relationship network won't be meaningful to you
until you first find your meaning in God.**

Here's the beautiful thing about this: God loves you for who you are. You don't have to perform for God in order to win his favor. The beauty and wonder of your life in Christ is that there's nothing you can do to earn the right to connect with God. All you have to do to begin your new life in Christ is to believe and receive the gift of salvation.

> God saved you by his special favor when you believed. And you can't take credit for this; it is a gift from God. Salvation is not a reward for the good

"What Is a 'Christian'?"

A Christian, a "fully devoted follower of Christ," is someone who ...
- *Believes* that the death and resurrection of Jesus Christ are sufficient to completely connect someone with God;
- *Has faith* that God's plan is best, both in this life and in eternal life;
- *Has repented* for offending God, and turned away from any lifestyle that is not pleasing to God;
- *Has determined* to live his or her life by the principles revealed in God's Word, the Bible.

"What a 'Christian' Is Not"

Don't believe everything you hear (especially on television) when it comes to Christianity. Don't reject God because you think it means you have to be ...
- *Fanatical.* God will never ask you to be weird and wild. All that God asks is that you are genuine.
- *Brain-dead.* God wants you to love him with your heart *and* your mind. Christianity can hold up to intellectual investigation.
- *Super Religious.* You don't have to give up your day job and move to a monastery. You don't even have to begin using "spiritual language." God wants you to be yourself as you connect with him.

things we have done, so none of us can boast about it. For we are God's masterpiece. He has created us anew in Christ Jesus, so that we can do the good things he planned for us long ago.

EPHESIANS 2:8-10

Once you have connected with God on a personal level, a whole new world will open up to you. It won't happen right away, but it will happen. As you learn more about your new life in Christ, you will learn to love God, and you will discover how important it is to truly love the people in your relationship network.

Follow God's example in everything you do, because you are his dear children. Live a life filled with love for others, following the example of Christ, who loved you and gave himself as a sacrifice to take away your sins.

EPHESIANS 5:1-2

As a growing child of God, you will begin to bear a resemblance to your heavenly Father because you will be imitating the personality qualities and values exhibited by Jesus Christ. Of course, you will need supernatural power, which God provides through the Holy Spirit (see John 14:15-17).

But when the Holy Spirit controls our lives, he will produce this kind of fruit in us: love, joy, peace, patience, kindness, goodness, faithfulness, gentleness, and self-control.

GALATIANS 5:22-23

Are you interested in taking your relationship to the next level? Here's how you do it. You ask God to work through you to show these qualities to others. As you do that, your entire relationship network will be strengthened because God will be in the middle of everything.

Real Life Essentials

We want to conclude this chapter on the meaning of your real life by giving you some real life essentials. What are these for? Think of them as fuel cells to keep you going and growing in Christ. The more consistently you connect with God (Essentials #1-5), the more love you will have for others (Essentials #6-8), the more you will trust God (Essential #9), and the more you will look forward to Christ's return (Essential #10).

Here are ten real life essentials for growing Christians.

1. Live to please God. As you get to know God better, you will love him more, and you will want to please him in all you do.

May the words of my mouth and the thoughts of my heart be pleasing to you, O Lord, my rock and my redeemer.

PSALM 19:14

2. Learn to worship God. Worship should be a natural expression of appreciation to God for who he is and for what he has done to save us. True worship is expressed in actions as well as in words.

> Come, let us worship and bow down. Let us kneel before the Lord our maker, for he is God. We are the people he watches over, the sheep under his care. Oh, that you would listen to his voice today!
>
> PSALM 95:6-7

3. Desire to pray to God. Prayer is the way we talk with God. There are no formalities involved, just a desire to converse with the most important person in your life.

> Pray at all times and on every occasion in the power of the Holy Spirit.
>
> EPHESIANS 6:18

4. Hunger for the Word of God. God talks to us through his Word, the Bible. Yes, he also speaks to us through the inner voice of the Holy Spirit, but you will hear his voice more clearly if you read the Bible consistently.

> You must crave pure spiritual milk so that you can grow into the fullness of your salvation. Cry out for this nourishment as a baby cries for milk, now that you have had a taste of the Lord's kindness.
>
> 1 PETER 2:2-3

5. Be willing to obey God. Just like you can do things to harm you physically, there are things you can do to harm you spiritually. A growing Christian will try to avoid the harmful stuff by obeying the good stuff God wants for us.

> And how can we be sure that we belong to him? By obeying his commandments. If someone says, "I belong to God," but doesn't obey God's commandments, that person is a liar and does not live in the truth.
>
> 1 JOHN 2:3-4

6. Get together with other Christians. A growing Christian needs to be around others who have a similar love for God. The best place to find other Christians is at church, where people meet to worship God, study the Bible, and care for each other.

And let us not neglect our meeting together, as some people do, but encourage and warn each other, especially now that the day of his coming back again is drawing near.

HEBREWS 10:25

7. Have a heart for others. One of the most important ways we can imitate Christ is to meet the physical needs of the poor, the defenseless, and the sick. A growing Christian has compassion for people who are unable to help themselves.

Dear children, let us stop just saying we love each other; let us really show it by our actions.

1 JOHN 3:18

8. Be concerned for the unsaved. As you grow in Christ, you will have a desire to share the Good News you have found with those who haven't yet connected with God on a personal level. As you live to please God, worship him, pray to him, and read his Word, the Holy Spirit will give you the power and the desire to tell others about him.

But when the Holy Spirit has come upon you, you will receive power and will tell people about me everywhere.

ACTS 1:8

9. Trust in God's grace. Never forget that God saved you by his grace, which means you have been given something you don't deserve. And it is his grace that keeps you going.

God saved you by his special favor when you believed. And you can't take credit for this; it is a gift from God.

EPHESIANS 2:8

10. Anticipate Christ's return. As much as you love your life, and as much as God wants to use you in the lives of others, you need to look forward to the day when Christ will come back to earth. As the old spiritual song goes, "This world is not my home, I'm just passing through." A growing Christian eagerly looks forward to the return of Christ when his eternal kingdom will be established.

But we are citizens of heaven, where the Lord Jesus Christ lives. And we are eagerly waiting for him to return as our Savior.

PHILIPPIANS 3:20

There you have it: the way to find the meaning of your real life. It doesn't matter what career path you take. You could be in finance, you could be in the communications industry, or you could be a student—God wants you to find your real life in him. Whether you are a computer expert, an athlete, or in sales—God wants to use you right where you are, to impact others for him. You could be an artist or a musician, or you may be skilled at building stuff—God made you and loves you and knows what's best for you.

As we conclude our book on your real life, we're going to take a look at how you can deepen your relationship with God by getting alone with him.

CHAPTER 12

When You Go Off-Line

Have you ever watched a kid play with one of those crazy remote-control toy cars that looks like a miniature dune buggy? (OK, admit it, you've played with one and you had a blast.) These screaming machines zip down the street and back, flipping and turning and crashing as you do your best to guide it with your hand-held controller. You have fun for about fifteen minutes, and then you notice something unsettling. Your Super Remote Control Buggy slows down as the batteries begin to run low on power. And then, no matter how hard you push the joystick with your weakening thumbs, the toy finally dies. You're out of power.

Not to worry. The buggy has a rechargeable battery pack (sold separately, of course). You simply remove the battery pack and plug it in for an hour or two, so it will be ready for another fifteen minutes of fun.

Remote-control vehicles aren't the only things we recharge. In fact, the rechargeable battery pack has become a staple in our high-tech world. If you don't admit to playing with toys, you would probably show us your notebook computer, your Walkman, your Palm Pilot, and your cell phone, all of

188 / Real Life Is a Contact Sport

which depend on rechargeable batteries. If you want to stay connected in today's world, you have to pay attention to all your batteries and make sure they are in a constant state of recharging. Otherwise your sophisticated devices are nothing more than expensive paperweights.

You can add one more device to your collection of battery-powered toys—*you*. No doubt you operate on a slightly higher level than a toy dune buggy, but you have a lot in common with the little gizmo. Just like the toy, you dash back and forth in a series of unpredictable maneuvers; you do flips and radical turns just to satisfy the instructions and demands of the people holding your remote-control joystick; and occasionally you crash at the end of the day because you've done more than you should. You're mentally, emotionally, and physically drained, and you need a recharge.

So you do those things that all of us do in order to recharge the batteries—you eat, read, watch TV, go to the movies (or whatever it is that relaxes you), go to Starbucks, and most of all, sleep. And amazingly, by the next day you're ready for another round of battery-powered dune buggy adventures.

Or are you? Haven't you forgotten something? You have recharged your mental, emotional, and physical batteries, but what about your spiritual battery pack? When's the last time you plugged your soul back into the Source of your spiritual power?

Going Off-Line With God

The principle of "going off-line" is essential to the long-term efficiency and survival of all machines. Whenever you need to recharge, repair, update, or upgrade a mechanical device, you have to power it down and take it out of circulation for a while.

The same goes for the physical, mental, and emotional dimensions of your body: you power down, you get away, you take yourself out of circulation, even if it's for a few minutes. There's no other way to keep up with the demands of your life, including the needs and expectations of the people in your relationship network—

- Family
- Friends

- Spouse
- Co-workers
- Difficult People
- Neighbors

In every chapter of this book, we have talked about the need to connect and the need to be deliberate about connecting with these people. Now we're suggesting that you build buffers into your relationships by disconnecting on a regular basis. And nowhere is that more important than in your spiritual life.

Back in Chapter 3 we said that God created us to be in relationship with him. As human beings, this is our first and most basic need. Without the dynamic presence of God in our real life, we are severely handicapped in every other dimension of our lives, especially our relationships with people. Conversely, as we work to strengthen our relationships with God, all of our people relationships become more meaningful and more satisfying. So as we close this book, let's look at ways to connect with God on a deeper level.

Getting Along With God by Getting Alone With God

In case you haven't noticed, God has always been a very active Supreme Being. He's not some disinterested observer who created the universe only to step back and watch it wind down. He's interested and involved in everything that goes on.

But don't let God's bigness and power prevent you from getting intimate with him. He isn't the Wizard of Oz, hiding behind a celestial curtain while playing with fire and smoke in order to frighten us mortals. Yes, God can split a mountain and cause the seas to roar, but that's not how he prefers to get our attention.

If you're waiting for God to get your attention by yelling, you might be waiting for a while. If you think God is going to take the initiative to set up a meeting with you by penciling your name in his heavenly Day Timer, think again. Remember, God is the perfect gentleman. He won't force himself on you. Instead, he's waiting for you to take the initiative. He's waiting for you to call out to him so he can answer you—not with fire and brimstone, but with a gentle whisper.

Be silent and know that I am God!

PSALM 46:10

"God Speaks to Elijah"

One of the more colorful characters in the Bible was the prophet Elijah. The Book of 1 Kings tells the story of a time when God told Elijah to stand on Mount Sinai and wait for him. As Elijah stood there by himself, a fierce windstorm hit the mountain, tearing rocks loose. "But the Lord was not in the wind." Then an earthquake shook the mountain. "But the Lord was not in the earthquake." After the earthquake, there was a mighty fire. "But the Lord was no in the fire. And after the fire there was the sound of a gentle whisper." And the Lord was in the gentle whisper. That's how he came to Elijah (1 Kings 19:11-13).

With just about everything else in our lives, we think we have to make a lot of noise and create a big ruckus in order to get attention. Not so with God. He's not going to yell at us, and neither does he want us waving our arms wildly at him, as if to say, "Over here, God, I'm over here! Pay attention to me!" God knows where we are, and he knows what we need. All we have to do is get quiet before the Lord and get ready to hear him speak to us. And the best way we know to do that is through the spiritual disciplines.

Be silent before the Lord, all humanity, for he is springing into action from his holy dwelling.

ZECHARIAH 2:13

The Secret World of Spiritual Discipline

In his classic book, *Celebration of Discipline*, Richard Foster writes that the "classical disciplines of the spiritual life call us to move beyond surface living into the depths." What are the spiritual disciplines? These are the activities of our spiritual nature that bring us into a closer relationship with God.

From the earliest traditions of the church, the spiritual disciplines have included Bible study, prayer, meditation, and solitude (we're going to look at these four in greater depth in just a minute). Simplicity, submission, and service are also spiritual disciplines, as are confession, worship, and celebration.

Don't make the mistake of believing that these spiritual disciplines are only for people who get paid to be spiritual. They are for everybody. Foster writes:

> We must not be led to believe that the Disciplines are only for spiritual giants and hence beyond our reach, or only for contemplatives who devote all their time to prayer and meditation. Far from it. God intends the Disciplines of the spiritual life to be for ordinary human beings: people who have jobs, who care for children, who wash dishes and mow lawns. In fact, the Disciplines are best exercised in the midst of our relationships with our husband or wife, our brothers and sisters, our friends and neighbors.

Like we said, we're going to talk about Bible study, prayer, meditation, and solitude. We're going to start with solitude, because each of the other disciplines is much more effective when you're alone with God than when you're with people. Yes, you can read the Bible, pray, and meditate in a group, but if church or a group Bible study is the only place you open God's Word, talk with God, and think about what God is saying to you, then you are denying yourself the opportunity and the privilege to go deeper with God on a personal level.

Solitude: He Knows You're Alone

"The purpose of silence and solitude is to be able to see and hear," writes Foster. Thomas à Kempis, the great fourteenth-century monk, wrote: "In silence and quiet the devout soul advances in virtue and learns the hidden truths of Scripture. There she finds a flood of tears with which to bathe and cleanse herself nightly, that she may become the more intimate with her Creator the farther she withdraws from the tumult of the world. For God and His holy angels will draw near to him who withdraws from friends and acquaintances."

As if we need more convincing, the greatest example of going off-line with God was no less than Jesus. With his built-in connection to God (being the Son of God and equal to God in every respect), you would think that Jesus didn't need to get away and get with God. But he did. Here are some of the situations in the Bible (pointed out by Richard Foster) when Jesus got alone to study, pray, and meditate:

- Jesus was alone for forty days and forty nights before he began his public ministry. At the end of this period of solitude, Satan tempted Jesus, who resisted his adversary by relying on the Word of God (see Matthew 4:1-11).
- Before choosing the twelve men who would be his disciples, Jesus went alone to a mountain to pray to God all night (see Luke 6:12).
- After his friend John the Baptist was beheaded, Jesus "went off by himself in a boat to a remote area to be alone" (Matthew 14:13).
- After he miraculously fed the five thousand, Jesus "went up into the hills by himself to pray" (Matthew 14:23).
- One day Jesus worked long into the night healing great numbers of diseased and demon-possessed people. "The next morning Jesus woke long before daybreak and went out alone into the wilderness to pray" (Mark 1:35).
- In the hours before Jesus was betrayed, leading to his arrest and eventual crucifixion, Jesus prayed by himself in the garden of Gethsemane (see Matthew 26:36-46).

Are you seeing a pattern here? Jesus worked as hard as any person ever has. The demands on his time were as great or greater than anything we will ever experience. The pressures he faced on earth were enormous. And yet he always made time to get alone with God.

"When's the Best Time and Where's the Best Place?"

There is no magic formula for *when* you should get alone with God. For some people, the early morning is best (these would be your morning people). Other people prefer a time in the evening (these would be people who hate the morning). The key ingredient seems to be *quiet*. Choose a time when the distractions of the day are at their minimum.

As for *where*, the operative word is *alone*. Set aside a place where you can "go away by yourself, shut the door behind you, and pray to your Father secretly" (Matthew 6:6). If your house is too noisy, go outside (notice how often Jesus got alone outside in remote places).

Bible Study: God's Word to You

OK, so you're alone, just you and the quiet and God. Now what do you do? Do you stare into space waiting for God to say something? Well, not exactly. We think a better plan would be to read God's personal message to you. That would be the Bible.

More than some ancient holy book full of thee's and thou's, the Bible is the dynamic Word of God, "full of living power ... sharper than the sharpest knife, cutting deep into our innermost thoughts and desires" (Hebrews 4:12). Do you want God to speak to you in a powerful way? Look no further than the Bible you already have.

Our suggestion is that you begin your off-line quiet time with God by reading the Bible. The benefits are incredible, as explained by this verse from the Bible:

All Scripture is inspired by God and is useful to teach us what is true and to make us realize what is wrong in our lives. It straightens us out and teaches us to do what is right. It is God's way of preparing us in every way, fully equipped for every good thing God wants us to do.

2 TIMOTHY 3:16-17

In our book, *Bruce & Stan's Guide to the Bible,* we found seven Bible reading benefits in this verse.

1. Motivation. "All Scripture is inspired by God ..." How much more motivation do we need? The Bible contains the very words of God, dictated by God (and written down by men) for our benefit. When you read the Bible, you will literally hear God speaking to you.

2. Instruction. "...and is useful to teach us what is true..." Do you want to know the truth about God and what he wants you to do? Do you want to know the truth about your life and your relationships? Read the Bible. Too many people rely on secondhand knowledge and totally skip the firsthand instruction available to us through God's Word. There's nothing wrong with good advice from well-meaning people. But never substitute the advice of others for God's firsthand instruction.

3. Detection. "... and to make us realize what is wrong in our lives." The Bible is like a mirror giving us an accurate picture of our lives and the things we are doing. It helps us detect harmful thoughts and actions.

4. Correction. "It straightens us out ..." We need to read the Bible every day, because even a small error, left uncorrected, can lead to huge problems later on.

5. Direction. "... and teaches us to do what is right." Not only does the Bible tell us what is wrong with our lives, but it also tells us the right things to do. More than a book of theory, the Bible gives us practical advice for life.

6. Preparation. "It is God's way of preparing us in every way ..." Isn't this great? God wants to prepare us for everything life throws at us. Whether it's at school, in our jobs, or in our relationships, the Bible gives us the information and inspiration we need to be effective.

7. Realization. "... fully equipped for every good thing God wants us to do." We have talked about ways to find purpose and meaning in our lives, and we've suggested that the only way to do that is to connect with God. Reading the Bible is the best way to connect with God, because it shows how God wants to equip us for the great stuff he wants us to do.

"How Do I Read the Bible?"

Anytime you read the Bible, you are going to benefit. But you will benefit even more if you read the Bible *regularly* and *systematically*. By regularly, we mean every day, if only for a few minutes. By systematically, we mean that you have a system. Read the Bible through in a year, a little each day (there are special Bible editions that will help you do this), or follow a Bible-reading plan around certain themes. The more disciplined you are in your Bible reading, the more you will get out of God's Word.

Prayer: Your Words to God

If the Bible is the primary way God talks to us, then prayer is the primary way we talk to God. Do you want to get God's attention? Do you want to engage the power of God in your life? There's no better way to do that than to pray. The Bible is very clear that we are to devote ourselves to prayer "with an alert mind and a thankful heart" (Colossians 4:2). We are to "pray at all times and on every occasion in the power of the Holy Spirit" (Ephesians 6:18). And we can be sure that when we pray, God will hear us (see Psalm 4:3).

God loves to hear us pray to him, but that's not why he asks us to pray. God wants us to pray because prayer is part of the process that he uses to get involved in our lives and the lives of others:

- Our eternal salvation involves prayer (see Romans 10:9-10).
- God's forgiveness of sins involves prayer (see 1 John 1:9).
- We gain spiritual strength through prayer (see Isaiah 26:3).
- God gives wisdom when we pray for it (see James 1:5).
- The best thing we can do for others is to pray for them (see Ephesians 6:18).

"How Should I Pray?"

This isn't a dumb question. The disciples asked Jesus the same thing, and he responded by giving them a pattern for prayer commonly known as the "Lord's Prayer" (you'll find it in Matthew 6:9-13). Here's an easy way to remember the elements of the Lord's Prayer that are important to your prayer life. Use the acronym ACTS:

A: Adoration
Praise God for how great he is.
C: Confession
Tell God you're sorry for the wrong things you've done.
T: Thanksgiving
Express your gratitude to God.
S: Supplication
Ask God to work in the details of your life and the lives of others.

You may also wonder how often you should pray. The Bible says to "pray at all times" (Ephesians 6:18), but that doesn't mean you have to walk around with your eyes closed (that could be hazardous to your health, especially if you're driving). It means that you have an attitude of prayer at all times. You're always connected to God through your thoughts and your heart. The time to be more systematic in your prayer life is when you are alone with God in your off-line quiet time each day.

Meditation: Taking Time to Think

Picture yourself alone in your off-line quiet time. You've read the Bible to hear from God through his Word, and you've prayed to God so he can hear from you. Are you done? You could be, but why not take a little extra time to just listen to God? In any conversation, listening is critical, and it's no different with God.

Are we telling you that if you listen, God is suddenly going to start speaking to you in an audible voice? No, that's not how God works. What he will do is speak through your thoughts through the Holy Spirit, who specializes in guiding us into truth (see John 16:13). But in order to hear the Holy Spirit, we have to be quiet and listen.

The Bible word for this process is "meditate." You may think that meditation means sitting in the yoga position as you chant mindless phrases. Nothing could be farther from the truth. In the Bible, meditate means to think about, ponder, and imagine what God has in store for you. The best analogy we have heard is a cow chewing its cud. After a cow eats, it brings up the partially digested food and chews on it some more. You'll never see a cow chewing its cud on the run. Usually she's lying down under a tree, away from the herd.

When you read the Bible and pray, it's like you are digesting God's Word into your life. When you meditate, you bring it up again and think about what God has said. The psalmist David put it this way:

I will study your commandments and reflect on your ways.

PSALM 119:15

When you build space into your off-line time with God to reflect on God's Word and God's ways, you will be amazed at what God says.

"The Art of Journaling"

Ever since people could write, they've been writing down stuff about God. Some of this stuff finds its way into books so others can read it, but most of the time it ends up in what is commonly known as a journal. Think of a journal as a record of your daily journey with God, and don't worry that someone's going to read it. This is between you and God. He's written a love letter to you (that would be the Bible), and you're simply writing back to him. Get a simple notebook or one of those blank books, and write at the conclusion of your off-line time. Don't worry about grammar or spelling (God doesn't care). Just write and be aware that God may be speaking to you through your own words.

Time to Get Started

It's hard to believe that we've reached the end of our little book on relationships. It may seem a little funny to be concluding with this chapter about you and God, but we hope you see what we're trying to do. You're going to run into people and establish relationships, whether you want to or not. You won't be able to avoid the contacts you make each day, but you can choose to be deliberate in building your relationships (at least that's what we've been trying to tell you).

Although we wouldn't recommend it, it is possible to arrange your life so you limit your contact with other people. No matter what you do, however, you are going to come in contact with other people. You can't avoid them, so we suggest you give serious consideration to how you are going to relate with them.

On the other hand, it is possible to avoid God. You don't automatically run into God in the course of your day. That's why you have to be deliberate about setting aside time for him. As important as your relationships with other people are to you, your relationship with God is even more important. He is the person you start with first, and the time to get started is now.

BIBLIOGRAPHY

Bickel, Bruce, and Stan Jantz. *Bruce & Stan's Guide to God*. Eugene, Ore.: Harvest House, 1997.

Bickel, Bruce, and Stan Jantz. *Bruce & Stan's Guide to the Bible*. Eugene, Ore.: Harvest House, 1998.

Cloud, Henry, and John Townsend. *Boundaries in Dating*. Grand Rapids, Mich.: Zondervan, 2000.

Crabb, Larry. *The Safest Place on Earth*. Nashville, Tenn.: Word, 1999.

Foster, Richard. *Celebration of Discipline*. San Francisco: HarperSanFrancisco, 1998.

Hahn, Todd, and David Verhaagen. *GenXers After God*. Grand Rapids: Baker, 1998.

Harris, Joshua. *I Kissed Dating Goodbye*. Sisters, Ore: Multnomah, 1997.

LaHaye, Tim. *Transformed Temperaments*. Wheaton, Ill.: Tyndale, 1993.

Lampman, Lisa Barnes, ed. *Helping a Neighbor in Crisis*. Wheaton, Ill.: Tyndale, 1999.

Littauer, Florence. *How to Get Along With Difficult People*. Eugene, Ore.: Harvest House, 1999.

McGinnis, Alan. *The Friendship Factor*. Minneapolis: Augsburg Fortress, 1979.

Magee, Robert. *The Search for Significance*. Nashville, Tenn.: Word, 1998.

Miller, Calvin. *The Empowered Leader*. Nashville, Tenn.: Broadman and Holman, 1997.

Shedd, Charlie W. *How to Know If You're Really in Love*. Kansas City, Kans.: Sheed, Andrews and McMeel, 1978.

Smith, Fred. *You and Your Network*. Mechanicsburg, Pa.: Executive, 1998.

Warren, Neil Clark. *Finding the Love of Your Life*. Colorado Springs, Colo.: Focus on the Family, 1998.

Wright, H. Norman. *Relationships That Work*. Ventura, Calif.: Regal, 1998.

ABOUT THE AUTHORS

Bruce Bickel quickly abandoned his fledgling career as a comedian because he wasn't very funny. Now he is a probate lawyer, so everybody expects him to be boring. Bruce lives in Fresno, California, with his wife, Cheryl. When he isn't doing lawyer stuff, he is active at Westmont College, where he has taught and serves on the Board of Trustees.

Stan Jantz is the father part of a father-son business that designs and maintains Web sites for companies and non-profit organizations. Stan lives in Fresno, California, with his wife, Karin. Stan is active in his church and is on the Board of Trustees at Biola University.

Bruce and Stan like to observe and comment on the culture around them. (It beats doing yard work and household chores.) They must be noticing something because they have written twenty books that have sold more than 1.3 million copies.

Some of their popular books include:
- *Real Life Begins After High School*
- *Bruce & Stan's Guide to God*
- *Bruce & Stan's Guide to the Bible*
- *Bruce & Stan's Guide to the End of the World*
- *God Is in the Small Stuff – and It All Matters*
- *God Is in the Small Stuff for Your Family*
- *God Is in the Small Stuff for Your Marriage*
- *God Is in the Small Stuff – Graduate's Edition*

Bruce and Stan would enjoy hearing from you. You can contact them with your praise, your criticism (be gentle), and your comments or questions by E-mail at: guide@bruceandstan.com. If you think they are worth the price of postage, you can send your letters and gifts to: P.O. Box 25565, Fresno, CA 93729.

Their Web site address is: **www.bruceandstan.com**. (Clever, huh?)